Huddersfield Mills

Newsome Mill with its clock-tower, a landmark in the district, as seen from the mill dam (*see Chapter Five*).

Huddersfield Mills

A Textile Heritage

Vivien Teasdale

Wharncliffe Books

First Published in Great Britain in 2004 by
Wharncliffe Books
An imprint of
Pen & Sword Books Ltd
47 Church Street
Barnsley
South Yorkshire
S70 2AS

ISBN 1 903425 77 8

A CIP catalogue record for this book is
available from the British Library

Typeset in Ehrhardt 10 on 12 point by
Mac Style Ltd, Scarborough, N. Yorkshire

Printed and bound in England by
CPI UK

Pen & Sword Books Ltd incorporates the Imprints of
Pen & Sword Aviation, Pen & Sword Maritime,
Pen & Sword Military, Wharncliffe Local History,
Pen & Sword Select, Pen & Sword Military Classics
and Leo Cooper.

For a complete list of Pen & Sword titles, please contact
Pen & Sword Books Limited
47 Church Street, Barnsley, South Yorkshire
S70 2AS, England
Email: enquiries@pen-and-sword.co.uk
Website: www.pen-and-sword.co.uk

Contents

Acknowledgements

So many people have provided so much help it is difficult to know where to begin, but especial mention must go to the following people.

Firstly I would like to thank the staff at West Yorkshire Archive Service in Kirklees, Bradford and Wakefield, and the staff at Kirklees Library, all of whom were unfailingly cheerful and supportive in my constant demands for books, documents and local knowledge; Stephen Carter at the Huddersfield Examiner Library; Hilary Haigh, University of Huddersfield Archivist; G Murphy and S M Stewart, who took the trouble to write to me about their experiences in textiles; and B Couchman, W Eastwood, M Sykes and the ladies of the Good Companions, Slaithwaite, who provided me with so much oral history of life in a textile mill.

My thanks go to C W Taylor of Taylor & Livesey; to Peter Johnson of W T Johnson & Co, Mr D Smith of Huddersfield Fine Worsteds, Ian Bell of Drake's Extrusions, James and Christine Haigh, Mrs M S Glendinning and W W Kenyon, who all provided information on and illustrations of their companies and mills; and to J L Brierley, Huddersfield Estate Co, H D Compass Tyres Ltd, M Mosley and Brierley Brothers Ltd, all of whom gave their time to show me around their mill buildings and explained so much about them.

I very much appreciated the help of C G Hobson, who allowed access to his considerable collection of mill memorabilia, and B D Moriarty, I Bell and S Whitwam, who also provided illustrations and much local knowledge.

The author would like to thank the following for their kind permission to reproduce photographs, prints and documents: Mr G Barber (pp. 94 upper, 109), Mr Ian Baxter (pp. 132 upper, 161), Mr J Bray (p. 110 lower), Brierley Brothers (p. 105 upper), Drake Extrusions (pp. 150, 152), Eddisons (p. 52), Ms E Ellam (p. 39 upper), English Heritage Crown copyright NMR (p. 135), Ms Sandra France (p. 40 upper), Mrs E Glendinning (pp. 53, 55), J & C Haigh (pp. 148 lower, 153, 154 both, 156, 157), Mr C G Hobson (pp. 24 lower, 73, 151), Mr Malcolm Howarth (p. 111 lower), *Huddersfield Daily Examiner* (pp. 58, 137), Huddersfield Fine Worsteds (p. 42), Mr W Kenyon (pp. 75 both, 76, 78 lower, 79, 81 both), West Yorkshire Archive Service (pp. 70, 77 upper, 78 upper, 90 lower, 91) and Mr Steve Whitwam (p. 140). The 25-inch maps appear with acknowledgement to the Ordnance Survey. All other illustrations are from the author's collection.

Pen & Sword Publishers have guided me through the (for me) difficult process of bringing this project to fruition and my thanks go particularly to Rupert Harding for answering so many questions and giving helpful advice in this.

Finally, my grateful thanks to family and friends who gave unstinting support and encouragement over the many months it took to research and write this book.

Whilst I have tried to reflect faithfully the ideas, feelings and information gained from all of the above and the various archives examined, any errors and omissions are, of course, my own.

Preface

This book charts the progress of some of Huddersfield's many entrepreneurs and early mills. I had to be selective and those described reflect a personal choice. I have not included some of the most influential, such as the Crowther family in the Colne Valley or the Brook family of Meltham, whose stories are well documented. Nor have I included some businesses whose history has been written at length, such as Brierleys of Turnbridge, Starkeys of Longroyd Bridge or Armitages of Armitage Bridge.

I have tried to give a flavour of the different branches of the textile trade – Huddersfield was not totally given over to wool or worsted, though they were always foremost. The mills themselves came about for different reasons and this is reflected in their structure and position in the landscape. I have aimed to include a range of mills, together with a brief look at the families from which the principal businessmen came. Nor did these men limit themselves to their mills. They took an active part in the making of the town of Huddersfield and the outlying townships, as they developed from small, parish-run villages to urban areas run by an elected metropolitan council.

Where were the women in all this activity? Political and social pressures prevented single women pursuing a career in management – even the overseers could not be women, as the male workers would object. But many workers in the mills were women – single, married and widowed. The mill owners' wives and daughters sometimes took an active part in the business, though usually in the background. But when the patriarch died, it was often his widow who kept the mill going. When the card maker John Sykes died, his widow Charlotte held the business together until their sons were of an age to take over. They eventually turned the firm into Europe's largest card clothing company (making the tiny hooks that covered the cards).

In 1834 when the Parliamentary Commission interviewed mill owners in the area, Mary Horsfall was running a scribbling and fulling mill in Slaithwaite after the death of her husband, as her eldest son was only 16. The wives and daughters of other mill owners were serving on Ladies' Committees, running homes for orphans or schools, and organising relief for the poor.

But the story is not just about wealthy families. The mills employed thousands of men, women and children. Those people's records are often the hardest to find, but their lives and aspirations influenced the development of the town, as well as that of early trade unions and political parties.

Vivien Teasdale

Glossary

Arkwright, Richard	in 1770 invented his 'frame', the first machine to produce warp yarn
blending	mixing grades together to get overall grade of wool
burling	picking over cloth to remove bits
carding	separating the fibres of raw wool using card combs, later mechanised by Arkwright; process included willeying
Cartwright, Edmund	in 1785 invented a mechanised weaving loom
combing	combing smooth the fibres of worsted cloth
Crompton, Samuel	in 1779 invented his 'mule', the first machine to produce warp and weft yarns
cropping	raising the nap on cloth, then cutting it short to improve the finish – once done with heavy shears, later by machinery
doubling	twisting threads together to form longer yarn
drying	tentering (stretching out, clear of the ground) in fields, later in drying sheds
felt	a soft fabric made from wool that has been pressed together
fettling	cleaning to remove dirt left after other processes
fine woollen trade	uses short staples (short fibres, giving lower quality)
fulling	pounding woollen cloth (not worsteds) in large troughs of warm water and soap, to make felted cloth
Hargreaves, James	in 1764 invented the 'Spinning Jenny', which produced weft yarn
healding	passing threads through healds (eyelets halfway down wires held vertically by battens at top and bottom)
Kay, John	in 1733 invented his flying shuttle: cloth could now be woven broader than a man's arm-span and faster than the weaver could pass the shuttle across manually
low woollen trade	re-uses waste material
mending	unpicking knots (made by the weaver joining new or broken yarn) and weaving in broken threads to be undetectable
milling	another name for fulling
mungo	re-used rags made from woven fibres
overlooking	superintend looms and their workers, repairing looms and doing quality checks on cloths

rag sorting	sorting rags into different colours and types for waste reclaimers or garnetters
scouring	scouring with Fuller's earth to remove oil and size
serge	twilled woollen fabric with very hard-wearing qualities
shoddy	re-used rags made from knitted fibres
sleying	passing every warp thread between reeds in centre of loom – reeds were cheap, smooth and just the right size – which held the warp to the fly or batten and kept threads in place; after each pass, the sley of reeds was pulled forwards and drove home the weft to make the cloth
slubbing	after carding, drawing the fibres out further and joining them end to end, often with a slight twist
spinning	twisting the fibres together to form a strong yarn
teasel	dried head of the teasel plant – it has small hooks, ideal for raising the nap without damaging the cloth
tenterhooks	hooks on which wet cloth was fastened to stretch and dry it
twill	twilled cloth is woven with a diagonal raised pattern
warp twisting	twisting in new warp to old to avoid having to heald and sley new yarn
warp	threads running along the length of woven cloth
warping	winding yarn onto warp mill to lay out threads in correct length/width/colours for the loom; the yarn is then sized with glue to strengthen it, dried and put on the loom
weaving	passing yarn threads under and over each other to form cloth
weft	threads running from side to side in woven cloth
willeying	beating dirty fleeces by rod, later by machine, to remove dirt and bits
woollen cloth	woven from uncombed wool yarns (where fibres lie in all directions); tends to have a fluffy surface
worsted cloth	woven from wool yarns that have been combed to make the fibres parallel; tends to have a smooth surface.
worsted trade	uses long staples, combed smooth (long fibres, giving higher quality)

Abbreviations

FCR	Factory Commission Report, 1834 [British Parliamentary papers; Factory Commission Inquiries 1834; Part ii, vol. 5, C1 No. 262]
YTD	Yorkshire Textiles Directory, 1910–1980 [various dates]

Chapter One
Origins

At one time, the Lord Chancellor of England sat in Parliament on a sack stuffed with wool, representing the source of much of the wealth of the country. That wool did not come from the northern counties, but from the downs, the west country and the south. Yet by the eighteenth century, that trade in wool was on the move and within a few short years had taken root in the north, in particular in the West Riding.

It was not a new industry to the area. The West Riding has always produced some wool, but this was a domestic industry. Coarse, poor-quality cloths known as kerseys – intended mainly for home use – were made, bought and sold in the small open markets of Halifax, Bradford and Leeds. Only around the York area were finer cloths made.

But the Industrial Revolution changed that. Huddersfield, which had been a small market town, found itself at the centre of a thriving industry.

Landscape
Huddersfield is the meeting-point for several narrow valleys. The water from numerous streams runs down the steep hillsides and the valleys funnel it into the

View across the Colne valley.

rivers Colne and Holme, which meet in Huddersfield, and the Fenay Beck. Their waters join the River Calder 3 miles (5km) north-east of Huddersfield. The valleys have few areas that can be turned to arable use, or even good grazing for cattle. Moorland tops are covered in rough heather and poor grazing, where even sheep have to be helped to survive.

But this inhospitable landscape is one of the reasons why the wool textile trade has thrived. There is no limestone here, so the water is soft and ideal for washing wool. Water also provided power to work the early fulling mills, and later nearby mines supplied coal to power the mills of the Industrial Revolution. Iron supplies were available for the machinery and the scene was set.

The narrow valleys prevented large-scale settlements, but scattered hamlets on the hillsides needed a central mill for corn and later for fulling. These mills were owned by the local landlords and had to be used by all. They were watermills, often found near a bridge, a place that people from the villages could easily reach with their goods.

Almondbury was originally a much more important place than Huddersfield, but the mill for its manor was at King's Mill – on the River Colne near Aspley – and eventually Huddersfield overtook the earlier settlement in size and importance. Holmfirth became a centre for the villages of Holmbridge, Holme and New Mill, whilst Milnsbridge served the same purpose for the villages of the Colne Valley.

View across the Holme valley.

The Textile Industry

The textile industry began in the cottages where it was often carried on alongside farming or other occupations. The clothier would buy raw wool, usually about 50–60lb (22–27kg); the poorest weavers could afford to buy only 14lb (6kg) whereas the richest would probably go further afield and buy large quantities of wool, often of better quality.

The raw wool would then be picked over by hand to remove the bits of vegetation and dirt, before being carded (combed out) and spun by the women of the family – hence the term 'spinster' for a single woman who earned her living by spinning wool, which the men of the household would then weave. Outside many cottages can still be seen the 'wuzzing' holes, where wet yarn was placed in baskets and hung on a stick, to be swung or 'wuzzed' round to dry.

An early spinning wheel.

After weaving, the fabric had to be cleaned of all the dirt and grease by soaking it in liquid ammonia, the commonest form of which was urine, and then it was taken to the fulling mill to be properly washed and scoured. Once dry, it was 'burled' to remove all the remaining bits of vegetation or dirt, before being returned to the fulling mill, where it was 'milled' to felt the fibres together.

It was then stretched out on 'tenterhooks' to its original length and shape. There was often controversy over this, because if it was stretched too much, the dried cloth could be sold as being a longer length, but it would shrink considerably when washed. The government appointed inspectors called ulnagers to measure cloth and attach a seal to prevent such cheating. The fabric produced was a rough 'kersey', narrow in width and natural in colour. Better cloth was produced in East Anglia or the west country, which were then the main textile areas.

Early fulling mills often later developed into scribbling mills, and eventually cloth-finishing mills or cropping shops, where the cloth was brushed with teasel cards to raise the nap, then cropped to give a better finish. Water power was used at first, but as early as the 1790s it was proving insufficient and mills using the Fenay Beck were installing steam engines to supplement the poor water supply.

Manpower – or sometimes horsepower – was also used. Once larger machines were invented, water power was needed and mills developed by the river. When steam power took over, the mills

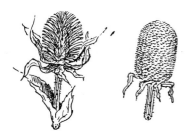

Teasel heads used in carding.

Taking-in doors, Golcar.

could be built anywhere, but the cost of transport played its part in their final location.

Smaller buildings were built, still attached to – or next to – the owner's home on the valley side. On the steeper-sided valleys, the top floor often had 'taking-in doors' facing the back road, where bundles of wool could be brought into the house directly to the loom.

The clothier spent the week weaving a single piece of cloth, which would then be taken from his home, perhaps high up on the moors, to the market. The better-off weavers would have a donkey or even a pony, but many shouldered their roll of cloth and walked however many miles were needed.

They went to Almondbury or, by the later seventeenth century, to Huddersfield. There, the churchyard walls were the only place to display cloth until the Cloth Hall was built in 1766. Buyers could carry away small pieces of cloth by packhorse and the early roads were rough tracks on the hilltops. Early turnpiked roads followed these tracks and ancient mileposts can still be seen isolated on the moors, but then came the canals which encouraged businesses to move down to the valley floor.

Whilst some weavers were able to continue and expanded their workshops along the valley sides, these small proto-mills were not able to compete with the larger ones

Milepost, Marsden Moor.

being built nearer to the new forms of transport. Improved roads and, later, railways followed the line along the valley floor and ribbon development of industry and housing followed.

Cotton also was produced in the Huddersfield area. Many of the early mills in the Colne Valley began as cotton mills, before converting to wool. The textile industry diversified, and some areas specialised. Fancy goods seem to have been produced mainly to the south-east, around Almondbury, Kirkheaton and Lepton, and out to Shepley, Cumberworth and Denby Dale. North-west, in Lindley and towards Outlane, velveteen and cords were produced, whilst woollen goods continued to be made in the Colne and Holme valleys.

In addition, there were silk mills, waste reclaimers, and even flax and linen merchants, who supplied the yarns for the cloth mixtures.

The Process

Wool is collected, then sorted. Each fleece is made up of different types of fibres and qualities. The wool is scoured to remove dirt and the sheep's natural grease. Lanolin is produced from this stage and is used in soaps, ointments and cosmetics.

For the woollen cloth industry, the raw wool is carded to tease out dirt. The fibres are mixed higgledy-piggledy and are shorter than those used in worsted. The yarn is then divided into slivers ready for spinning. Originally done by hand, carding was mechanised early in the development of the cotton industry.

Worsted yarns are washed and dried, then combed. This separates out the short fibres or noils, and ensures that the fibres are smooth, straight and lying parallel. The long fibres are wound into 'tops' ready for spinning, which can be used for different purposes.

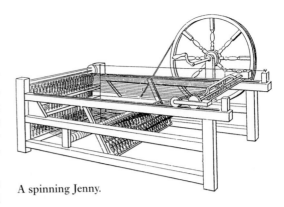

A spinning Jenny.

The early spinning machines invented by Hargreaves could only produce yarn suitable for weft, whilst Arkwright's frame, invented a few years later, produced warp yarn. It was Crompton's Mule, invented in 1779, which produced yarn suitable for either warp or weft, that allowed large-scale production of yarn. These machines all began in the cotton industry, but the wool industry was quick to see their advantages and adapt them to their needs.

Yarns can then be woven. Small hand looms were used in the home, and some homes had two or three looms on the top floor where the light was best. Cloth woven with complicated designs were called 'jacquard' and could be produced using specially punched cards that controlled which threads were raised for the weft yarn to pass through. Weaving was speeded up by the invention of Kay's 'flying shuttle' but it was not fully mechanised until Cartwright's inventions at the end of the eighteenth century.

The completed cloth then has to be 'finished'. This includes examining for faults and mending any breaks in the threads, before putting the cloth through a series of processes to stabilise it and to alter the final feel. For example, the nap may be raised by brushing with teasels or wire brushes, and this nap is then 'cropped' short. Cropping can be done on wet or dry cloth to give different finishes.

Wet cloth has to be dried. Originally this was done by stretching it on 'tenterhooks' – lines of which could be seen on the hillside – but, later, drying sheds or rooms near the boiler-house were built.

Cloth may be dyed at this stage, although sometimes it is done earlier. The chemical industry also developed in this area as a direct result of the needs of textile manufacturers.

Nineteenth Century

Initially the cloth had been sold in the Cloth Halls, but with the growth of the fancy weaves, manufacturers needed to keep their patterns more securely. Consequently, they began to display their goods in rooms at inns, later developing their own warehouses in the centre of Huddersfield where buyers could visit. Most of the larger enterprises also had their own London representative, who acted on their behalf in selling cloth to the merchants.

Later on, firms often sent members of the family to London or abroad to represent their interests, or employed commercial travellers to undertake this task. Cloth Halls

Clock Tower from the Cloth Hall, Huddersfield.

gradually fell out of use and were often demolished. The clock from Huddersfield Cloth Hall is now in the grounds of the Tolson Museum.

Twentieth Century

The textile industry has seen many ups and downs but has steadily declined over the years, both in terms of people employed in the industry and in the value of its exports. Cheaper imports, and businesses' ability to switch production to other countries where labour is cheaper, have forced the amalgamation or closure of a large percentage of Britain's textile firms. Some have responded by switching to other fibres, producing synthetic fibres or specialising in high-quality, niche-market fabrics, though many are still struggling.

Chapter Two
The Lindley Ridge

This extends westwards towards the Pennines, and is followed by the old turnpike route towards Manchester. From the town centre, Trinity Street climbs up onto the Lindley Ridge, leading to Marsh, Oakes, Quarmby and Lindley itself. On the north slopes are Edgerton and Birkby; to the south is Paddock in the Colne valley. The ridge continues by Outlane, beyond which lies Scammonden, which was home to some of the earlier mills in the area. The ridge borders and overlooks the Colne Valley, but it has no major streams or rivers to cut deep valleys. There were fewer mills here and they tended to be later mills, concentrating on the fancy woollen trade.

View across Milnsbridge.

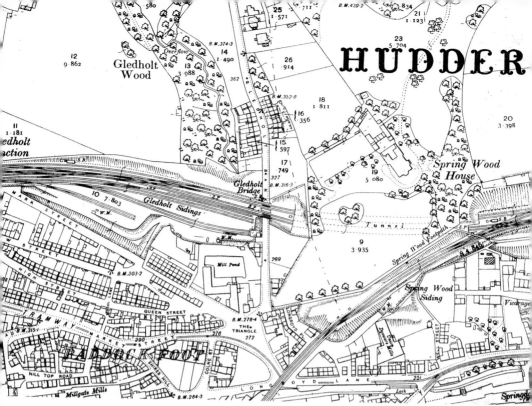

Ordnance Survey map 1907: scale 25″ to 1 mile.

Gledholt Mill

This is a good example of a mill that was in use continually over a long period of time, but was not associated with any one business for very long. Consequently, its origins and history are difficult to discover.

It is possible that there was a mill in this area in the sixteenth century, when there is a reference to a fulling mill at Paddock Foot, but this is more likely to have been further down, nearer the river. The mill at Triangle, Paddock, has been variously known as Pedley's Factory or Mill[1] and Paddock Mill[2] before it got its current name of Gledholt Mill, but there were other mills in Paddock Foot and it is sometimes difficult to work out which mill is meant.

Certainly, in 1818 Thomas Allen & Sons[3] seem to have been in Gledholt, listed as merchants and manufacturers, and they appear again in Baines' 1822 Trade Directory, which also includes John Bradley at Pedley Mills, Paddock. Thomas Pedley had his business in the mill that took his name, though his main residence seems to have been in London.

Other textile businesses in the area include William Thornton and John Tyre as merchants at Paddock Foot, with Joseph Armitage as both merchant and manufacturer. William Armitage is described as a scribbling and fulling miller of Paddock Foot, whilst Thomas Rushworth is a cloth dresser. Yet by 1851 the Trade Directory does not refer to Paddock Foot at all, but lists businesses in Paddock. The directory of 1857 shows James Haigh, cloth dresser, was at Pedley's Mill, as were John Bradley, a scribbling and fulling miller, and J Hepworth, a manufacturer of fancy goods.

An interesting variation occurred in 1864 when it was referred to as Pidley's Mill, but this is probably just a mistake. At this time two firms seem to have been there – William & Henry Crosland and Woodhead Bros – who were both manufacturers. W & H Crosland remained longest in the mill, subletting rooms to Alan Brook Haigh, a cord manufacturer, and to John Mellor of Fenton Square, an Angola yarn spinner and scribbler.

Paddock

Many of the houses in and around Paddock were built 'back-to-back' in blocks of four, with a narrow, dark passage between blocks. There was only one entrance/exit for each house, which usually consisted of one room downstairs for living/cooking and one or two bedrooms upstairs. There were no toilets, any 'night-soil' being collected by horse and cart each day.

Because of the steepness of the hillsides round about, some houses were built on top of each other, one family occupying the lower two floors, with a different family on the top two floors. Until the late nineteenth century, some handloom weaving was also carried out in these houses, which must have been exceptionally cramped and smelly from the greasy wool. Beds were merely curtained off from the living area, or sometimes squashed in around the looms, which were housed upstairs.

Both men and women were involved in weaving, with young children to help them – child labour was not invented with the factories, but at least at home the child could rest when necessary. Food was often an oatmeal porridge, or potatoes with a few vegetables or pig's trotters.

Home workers would often earn only 9 or 10s. (45–50p) per week, out of which they would have paid 3 or 4s. (15–20p) for rent. Workers in the mills usually had a slightly higher income, because children could earn a wage too. As a family their earnings could be as much as 14 or 15s. (70–75p).

Fire

Any mill was at risk from fire, so it must have been even more worrying if the building was used by many firms. In July 1872 there was a major fire at Gledholt. A young man employed by A B Haigh was on his way home when he saw smoke and flames from a room used by W & H Crosland. At first he tried to enter the room to put out the fire but was beaten back by the smoke, so he went to raise the alarm.

Fire engines from James Crosland & Sons arrived first and began pumping with water from the mill reservoir. Other engines arrived from a variety of places – the Liverpool, London and Globe insurance company, who insured the mill; Henry Crowther & Sons; Messrs Lockwood, Kaye executors; Huddersfield Corporation; George Crosland & Sons; John Brooke & Sons of Armitage Bridge; and Armitage Brothers of Milnsbridge.

In the event only four of the engines were used, but most engines turned out for mill fires because of the risk to other buildings nearby and as a precaution – no-one ever knew when they would be the ones needing help.

The roof of one of the wings of the five-storey building 'fell in with a terrific crash' and the people in the area 'thronged the roads and the hillside near the reservoir at the back of the mill' to get a better view. As long as they weren't at risk, it must have been quite exciting to hear the wood crackling and snapping, to see the flames leaping high and watch the sparks, like fireworks, spraying upwards as the roof collapsed. In all, over £8,000 of damage was done but, whilst the mill buildings were fully insured, not all the machinery and contents were.[4]

It is not really surprising that, the following year, further advertisements appeared for the sale of machinery from both John Mellor's business and that of W & H Crosland, who were forced into liquidation.[5]

The mill was rebuilt and later gave a home to E H Sellers & Co, and also T & H Whitehead. These two firms got together to give their workforce the traditional 'treat' in 1882[6] when they provided a party in one of the rooms. Warehouses were often the largest covered spaces available and the mill workers would clear the centre, sweep up and sometimes decorate the room with paper garlands. Tables were set up and food brought in. Usually a local band would entertain, with singing and dancing. Often the entertainment would come from the mill workers themselves, forming singing groups and bands.

Plan of Pedley Mill

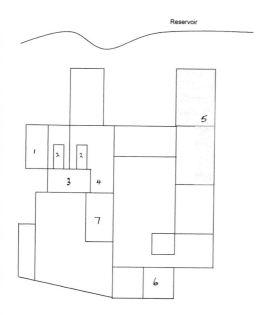

Reservoir

A major fire occurred again in 1894 early on Sunday 22 September.[7] The report describes the section of the mill as '12 windows long, 3 windows wide and 4 storeys in height'. The fire started this time in the bottom room, which was being used for storage by James Henry Firth of Paddock. The fire was spotted by PCs Garside and Wharf who raised the alarm.

This must have been in the early days of telephone as readers were informed that a 'telephonic message was got through to the [fire] station from Mr Lawton's spinning mill'. The fire spread quickly and became so hot that water had to be sprayed on nearby houses to save them, but even so they bore the marks of the fire in blistered woodwork. The plan

Key
1   Engine Room
2   Boiler
3   Stoke House
4   Steps
5   Burnt down in September 1894
6   Counting House
7   Leased to Holroyd & Co

Sketch of Pedley's Mill from survey dated 1891.

of the mill, drawn up in 1891, was amended to show which areas burnt down in this fire. These were never rebuilt.

Eventually, as before, the roof tumbled in and the building was gutted, but the offices at one end of the building – which were used by Paddock Labour Club – were saved. Part of the problem had been the gas pipes melting and the escaping gas fuelling the fire even further. Although the building was insured and was therefore able to be rebuilt, Firth's were insured for only half their loss, which was estimated at £2,000.

Later Use

By 1900 Gledholt Mill was used by Joseph Haigh, a dyer, who would have required large vats of dyes, boilers and chemicals for his business, with massive iron-wheeled trolleys to trundle the wet cloth about. Another part of the mill, probably on another floor, was the business of William Siswick & Sons,[8] who were waste dealers.

Although Batley and Dewsbury are the principal places associated with the 'shoddy and mungo' aspect of the textile trade, there were also waste reclaimers, or garnetters, in and around Hudders-field. Old cloths and garments can be 'opened up', torn apart and the fibres reworked. Sometimes the old fibres are mixed with virgin wool – though not usually the finest wool, but the noils or short fibres left over from worsted combing.

Trolley used in dyehouse.

Although the two phrases are often interchange-able nowadays, shoddy refers to fibres obtained from knitted cloths and mungo is fibres from woven cloths. The fibres need to be sorted into colours, to be sold in bundles of the same colour. Reused wool is not generally redyed but used as it is, giving a mottled or tweed effect.

Siswick's later moved elsewhere, and their place was taken by J Hinchcliffe & Co, who were also 'waste openers and pullers'. When Hinchcliffe and partners ceased business in 1909,[9] the items sold from the mill included an 18″ rag machine, a 60″ garnett machine and other equipment, such as weighing machines; a 42hp Crossley Otto-cycle gas engine, a 'W' type steam boiler and 30,000lb in raw material of worsted, stockings, serge, flannel and cloth, in blue, black, brown, white and mixed.

In the mill at the same time were A Shaw & Co, who were woollen and worsted spinners and manufacturers, probably on a commission basis for other companies.

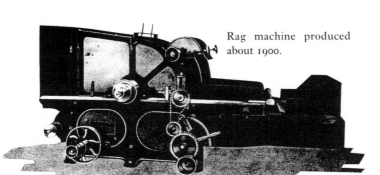

Rag machine produced about 1900.

The firm of Lockwood & Keighley – who won a prize medal for excellence of manufacture in woollen cords and velveteens at the

Great Exhibition of 1851 and made patent woollen cords, velvet and leather cloths, chiefly for trousers[10] – used the mill between 1910 and 1970.[11] Their principal base had been at mills in Upperhead Row in Huddersfield for many years but, after that was destroyed by fire, they moved to Gledholt Mills about 1910. They had 50 looms right up to 1971.

They were not the only firm there, nor was the mill always used purely for textile purposes. In September 1919 there appeared an advertisement for a sale from Gledholt Mills.[12] Messrs Quarmby & Sons were giving up business in the timber trade and their catalogue included timber and a Crossley gas engine of 15½hp, together with a circular saw and benches. The mill is described as a three-storey mill, with the ground floor divided for offices with desk, cupboard and upholstered stool,

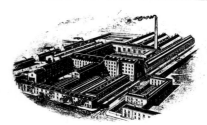

Letterheading of Lockwood & Keighley Ltd.

but also with shafting, pullies and so on, plus saw-benches and machinery.

The engine-house included a partition with 15½hp 'O' type gas engine with two flywheels, cast-iron driving pulley, two galvanised water tanks and pipe connections, with silencer by Crossley Bros Ltd. The other two floors contained benches, chopping machines, other equipment and timber.

The Hoyle group later bought the mill and a small amount of cloth was produced, but in 1961 production there was closed down and they transferred the thirty workers to other manufacturing premises in the group.[13] The mill was the smallest of the four mills owned by Hoyles and the only work carried on there was carding, spinning and weaving.

In November 1961 there was a 'farewell' celebration in the mill. Most of the workers felt they were part of a family because there were so few of them. Thomas Sykes, a scribbling engineer who had forty-two years' service with the firm, received a clock. It was presented by Willie Waite, another worker, who had been at Gledholt Mill since Hoyles began there in 1923.

Just twelve months later,[14] Hoyles were able to reopen the mill, taking on an extra fifty operatives for carding, spinning, weaving, warping and mending processes,

Gledholt Mill.

which were to be carried on there. This optimism didn't last as, by the end of 1963, two other mills in the group – Quarmby Clough and Gosport – were both closed[15] and parts of Gledholt Mill were leased to other businesses, including Taylor & Livesey of Ramsden Mills in Golcar. They used the mills for the knitting of double-knit jersey fabrics for ladies' outerwear.

It was later bought by Mr Harry Dyson and is now leased to Compass Tyres for storage. The old mill building of four storeys (with a small attic at top) still has the original timbered roofing beams and floorboards, now in very poor condition. The later extension to the building was three storeys high.[16] It originally looked out over a millpond, now filled in, and the bricked-up windows are below ground level. The pond area is now a car park/yard.

Portland Mills

Rowland Hall & Co

One of the main families involved in the textile industry around the Quarmby/Lindley area from the mid-nineteenth century onwards was the Hall family. It included Abraham Hall & Sons, John Hall & Sons and William & Joseph Hall.

Rowland Hall is known to have been a woollen manufacturer operating from the Wells Factory in Northgate, Huddersfield, in 1853 when the firm of John Hall & Sons was also there.[17] In 1856 he seems to have leased or bought land in Lindley, but there is no reference to mills in the lease.

The names of the fields he bought – Wellfield, Round Field, Hoyle Lane Close, Near Five Day Work and The Virginia[18] – were preserved in the names of streets built around this time, so it seems likely that Rowland Hall was responsible for building the nearby Portland Mills of the same date.

Ordnance Survey map 1907: scale 25″ to 1 mile.

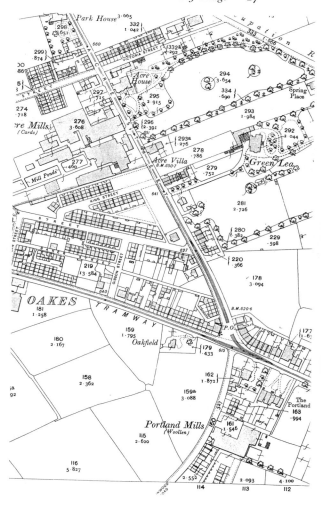

He continued at Wells Factory in Huddersfield until the early 1860s, when he moved to Portland Mills, referred to as 'Portland factory'.[19] He later went into partnership with Joseph Dyson of Lindley, and William Haigh of Longwood, to form the Foreign Mungo & Shoddy Dealers. They leased back the land and buildings that included Portland Mills.

The household in Portland House at this time consisted of two families. The Arrols were a Scottish family who had come down to work and manage one of the local mills. William Dawson, who shared the house, was a bank cashier, but his wife and stepdaughters obviously carried on some other business. An advertisement appeared in the paper, saying that:

> Mrs Dawson and the Misses Ellis beg to announce that the duties of their establishment will be resumed on the 28th of July.[20]

Unfortunately, it does not record just what the duties were!

About 1868, though, it is James Hall who is listed as being at Portland Mills, as shoddy merchant. His address is also given as

Portland House.

Portland House, whilst Rowland Hall is given no address at all, simply being referred to as fancy woollen manufacturer.[21] Whether he was ever actively involved in the shoddy and mungo business, or whether he merely provided finance, is not certain.

It is 1873 before Rowland Hall becomes definitely associated with Portland Mills, though now he is listed as an 'Angola yarn and fancy woollen manufacturer'.[22] In 1877 further mortgages were taken out on the mill buildings, to help finance the business or possibly to buy Portland House, as this became his address about this time.[23]

As usual, Rowland Hall was not alone in the mills. During the 1860s Joseph Hoyle, having been refused an overlooker's job at Quarmby Clough Mill, 'got a set of machines and installed them in Portland Mills, Lindley and increased these machines to two sets'.[24] He went on to become one of the foremost textile manufacturers in the area, moving into Prospect Mills and eventually purchasing Quarmby Clough Mill, Milnsbridge, Gledholt Mills at Paddock and Gosport Mills in Outlane.

Another firm associated with Portland Mills was Messrs John Haigh & Co,[25] who went bankrupt in 1866. That October the 'scribbling and fulling machinery' – mules, spindles and so on – was put up for sale. The following year another advertisement appeared for the sale of machinery from Portland Mills; this time it belonged to Thomas Haigh.[26] Many businesses came and went in quite a short period of time; and mills, or rooms in them, changed hands frequently.

In 1866 Samuel Mitchell, a card manufacturer of Honley, brought an action against Samuel Beaumont, manufacturer of Portland Mills, Lindley, for £20 7s. 5d. (£20.37), the value of some cards that had not been paid for. He won his case and an order was made for the full amount. The cards were used in the manufacture of worsted yarn. Originally they were made from teazle heads; later, wire-based ones were also produced, though they proved not as effective as the natural type.

The year 1883 brought an unexpected tragedy to the mills. Huddersfield Corporation had recently installed tramways on many roads, one of the most popular routes being that from the town centre up to Lindley. However, one day the tram appears to have run out of control on Trinity Street. The newspaper reported that:

Early spinning machine.

the force with which the car came down West Parade was something terrific. The engineer rang his bell, and the excitement was intense ... The females shrieked and indeed several of the male passengers did the same.[27]

It was hardly surprising that there was considerable shrieking – several passengers were thrown out of the tram, the top deck of which was open-air. One of the men on the top deck was Rowland Hall, who was badly injured and died of his head wounds. The inquest suggested that the driver had not used his brakes correctly but there is no indication that anyone was formally considered 'to blame' or that compensation was paid by the corporation.

Also injured in this incident, though not fatally, were Jane, wife of Frederick Peckett of Lindley, and Helena, her daughter, aged 6. The two families must have known each other because Jane's son Willie eventually married Rowland Hall's youngest daughter, Frances Emmeline.

F Peckett & Sons

Frederick Peckett was the eldest son of James and Hannah Peckett[28] of Shelley, where James was a 'fancy weaver'. He and Hannah (*née* Peace) brought up the children in what was then open countryside, with holidays at their grandparents' farm in Cumberworth.[29] The Peace family went on to become mill owners in the Denby Dale area and were comparatively wealthy, so Frederick was able to receive some education and training.

In 1858 he married Jane Gelder in Kirkburton Church[30] and eventually the family moved to Primrose Hill in Newsome. The Huddersfield Directory and Year Book for 1873 lists him as a designer living there, before the family moved to Longwood and finally to Lindley.

He was a staunch Baptist and took an active part in church life. As a Trustee in 1876,[31] he helped buy land on which to build the church at Primrose Hill. It was an association continued throughout his life and followed by his family, both at Primrose Hill and later at Salendine Nook Baptist Church, where many of the family are buried.

Fred worked originally as designer and manager for Messrs Thomson & Dodds but was also a designer at Huddersfield Mechanics' Institute, eventually becoming Head of Textile Designs. Many of the early teachers at these institutes were mill owners or managers, who were actively involved in improving the training opportunities for youngsters coming into the industry.

Fred Peckett was offered a similar post at the Yorkshire College at Leeds but refused this.[32] In 1875 he went into partnership with Charles Smith as Smith & Peckett of Prospect Mills, Longwood, until this partnership was dissolved and he helped set up the firm of Smith, Peckett & Co of Colne Vale Mills, Milnsbridge,[33] with Joseph Smith and James Calverley.[34]

A branch of this firm was opened at Portland Mills in 1879, but Frederick later started his own business, eventually forming the limited company of Fred Peckett & Co Ltd with his sons, Henry, Hedley and William.

Huddersfield Mechanic's Institute opened 1883.

The mill was four storeys high, plus a number of sheds. Later, a second mill of two storeys was added. The larger mill contained eight sets of carding and scribbling machines, finishing machinery and power looms, whilst the smaller mill had 300 spindles, scouring and milling work, beaming, twisting and finishing departments. Two engines fed by a large boiler supplied the power for both mills.

Industries of Yorkshire (Anon.) says that

Fred Peckett started life in a very unpretentious way and has worked his way up from humble beginnings, by downright earnest application, to his present prosperous position in which he enjoys the respect and confidence of a large circle of friends in private and commercial life.

By 1880 he had amassed sufficient wealth, or perhaps confidence, to invest in property. Although he had moved to Cliffe End at

Finishing & lustring machine.

Part of Portland Mill still standing and in use.

Lindley, he began buying houses in Shelley – where his family had originally lived – and later property in Lindley.[35]

In 1890 Fred bought the mills[36] on Reinwood Road. Apart from one small warehousing area, these have since been demolished. The deeds show that the mills originally covered 12,399 sq. yd (10,365 sq. m) and stood three storeys high. The complex included offices, store rooms, engine-house, boiler-house, weaving shed of two storeys, a long [that is, tall] chimney and a stable block for two horses. Fred also bought all the machinery and gearing, as well as the reservoir for the mill.

Letterheading of Fred Peckett & Sons.

CONTRACTORS TO HIS MAJESTY'S GOVERNMENT

Fredk. Peckett & Sons Ltd.

FANCY WOOLLEN MANUFACTURERS

Portland Mills, LINDLEY, near Huddersfield

TELEGRAMS: "PECKETTS, LINDLEY." Code, 5th Edition A B C   TELEPHONE No. 235

WAREHOUSE:
MARKET STREET (Attendance on Tuesdays and Fridays)   All Communications to be addressed to PORTLAND MILLS, LINDLEY

—— SPECIALITIES: ——

**Fancy Woollens and Worsteds   Overcoatings
Trouserings   Cap Cloths   Coverts   Army Cloths**

Orders executed direct by Cash Payment against Bill of Lading, or through the usual buying channels.   Samples sent to responsible Buyers with reference.
Please send copy of order when buying through Merchants.

FABRICANTS D'ÉTOFFES DE LAINE FANTAISIE.	FABRICANTES DE LANA DE FANTASIA.
Spécialités :	Especialidades :
Peignés et etoffes fantaisie, Etoffes pour pantalons et pardessus, pour casquettes, paletots et uniformes pour l'armée.	Lanas de Fantasia y Estambres, Paños para Gabanes, Géneros para Cortes de pantalon, Paños para Gorras, Paños lisos para Sobretodos, Paños para el Ejercito.
Commandes exécutées directement avec payement au comptant contre connaissement ou par les intermédiaires habituels. Echantillons envoyés à tout acheteur muni de références. Prière de nous adresser duplicata de toute commande faite par l'entremise des marchands.	Los pedidos se ejecutan directamente mediante pago al contado contra conocimiento ó por medio de casas exportadoras. Se envien muestras a compradores de responsabilidad con referencias. Sirvase enviar copia del pedido cuando se compre por mediación de comerciantes.

FABBRICANTI DI LANE A FANTASIA.

Specialità :
Lane a Fantasia e Filati, Stoffe per Cappotti, Stoffe per Pantaloni, Panni per Berrette, Coperte, Panni per Militari.

Ordini eseguiti direttamente mediante pagamento contante contro polizza di carico ossia per mezzo delle vie solite ai compratori. Campioni si mandano a serii compratori con reference complacevoli mandare copia commissione comprando per mezzo negozianti.

At the same time, he bought land at Firs Plantation, possibly as a 'job lot' or as speculation. Later he raised further finance via mortgages on 'land at Longwood' so this may have been the same land used as security.

The next generation included his sons, Hedley, Henry and Willie (named after an earlier William who had died in infancy), who all began their apprenticeship working with him in his business.

Henry was educated at the Huddersfield Mechanics' Institute, winning prizes for his work and eventually becoming a pupil teacher at the Lockwood Mechanics' Institute, just as his father had been a teacher at the Huddersfield Institute. He was a great music lover, being secretary to the Lindley Choral Society, on the committee of the Huddersfield Choral Society and Vice President of the Glee and Madrigal Society.

Hedley too was actively involved in the local community, being elected to the council in 1913 for Marsh Ward and continuing to serve for many years. He lived in Braeside, Blacker Road, Edgerton, before moving to Portland House in Lindley. He was appointed one of the governors of the Technical College.

He also served on the committee of the Lindley Mechanics' Institute, being involved in 1897 in the purchase of 618 sq. yd (516 sq. m) of land known as Sun Croft Close in Lindley on which to build the Institute.[37] Later, some of the land had to be sold to Huddersfield Corporation so they could widen the main road in the village. This building has now become the library and is being renovated. Hedley's interest in education also saw him involved with Longwood Grammar School.[38] Despite his mainly Baptist background, he is buried in St Stephen's Church in Lindley.

In November 1906 the mills suffered the ever-present hazard of fire, which did £400 of damage when fluff in the willeying room caught fire in the gas jet. Although it took under an hour to extinguish, 2,000lb (908kg) of bales were damaged. Fortunately, the amount was covered by insurance and the fire was confined to the old part of the mill. The following year a new mill was built.

In 1932 Portland Mills were bought by Sir Emmanuel Hoyle, a descendent of the Joseph Hoyle who had started out there seventy years previously. The mills were then sold to Rycroft & Co of Bradford, who joined with Messrs Filaturs de Delhain of Belgium to form the Anglo-Belgian Textile Company.

Many textile firms in the area relied on importing fancy yarns to include in their cloths but the government imposed tariffs on these types of yarns. As a result, some had to withdraw designs from their cloth ranges, so the new company intended to fill this gap by producing yarns similar to the continental type in a building which they described as 'highly suitable for the purpose being well arranged, adequately lighted and ideally suited for obtaining the necessary labour'.[39]

Although it was stressed that the new company would not be competing with local woollen spinners, as they were aiming at a different section of the trade, they did also produce white yarn to be used for cricketing flannels

Trade unions had early become involved in the textile industry. The Power Loom Tuners' Union records of 1920 show that Fred Peckett & Sons Ltd had 80 looms, tuned by union members Shaw Haigh and William Sykes.[40] This was an important job since it was essential that the looms were in continuous operation. Later, the National Union of Textile Workers tried to obtain jobs for their unemployed members with the Anglo–Belgian group, but this seems to have been unsuccessful as the vacancies had already been filled.

Records for the mills show that it had 80 looms and 5,000 spindles throughout the life of the two firms, but by 1970 production had declined. The firm was still associated with Joseph Hoyle & Co of Prospect Mills, Joseph Hoyle being Managing Director of both companies.

The decision was made to transfer all remaining business to Prospect Mills and its more modern plant, together with as many of the workpeople as possible. The mill finally closed in August 1970.[41] Housing now covers the site of the mill, though Portland House itself has been transformed into a children's nursery.

Wellington Mills

These massive mills – which, when built, would have dominated the landscape – sit just at the top of the rise from the centre of Huddersfield, on the way out towards what is now the M62 to Manchester.

They were built at Oakes about 1864 and at one time occupied by George Walker, woollen manufacturer, who was associated with the Walkers of Plover Mills on the same road in Lindley. An earlier map shows Plover Mills' dyehouse on the land now occupied by Wellington Mills, so it is probable that the dyehouse was either demolished or extended when the mills were erected.

Wellington Mills.

The Walker family mansion, Park House, was offered for sale at this time, together with cottages and land in Lindley. George Walker appears to have got himself into financial difficulty and the mills and much of the adjoining property were auctioned in 1864:[42]

> Valuable freehold property at Lindley. To be sold by Auction by Mr Benjamin Thornton at the Queen Hotel, Huddersfield on Tuesday the 5th day of April 1864 at Six o'clock for seven pm prompt (unless previously disposed of by private contract), the following FREEHOLD MILLS, LANDS AND MESSUAGES lately the property of Mr George Walker of Lindley, woollen manufacturer ...
>
> Lot 1 All that Capital Stone-built MILL called Wellington Mill, five stories high, and upwards of 44 yards in length, and 14 yards in width, with the long Chimney, Engine house, Boiler house, Fire proof Teazing room, Waterhouse, one story high, formerly used as a weaving shed, Press Shop and Tenter Stove, Counting house, Teazle room and Waterhouse over the same sheds and other conveniences, with three Closes of LAND adjoining thereto, called Near Foulton and Far Sparks, also, all that Large Reservoir constructed on a portion of the said close, called Far Sparks, with the Cast Iron Cooling Trough, on the bank and outlet pipes and valves belonging thereto.
>
> Also, the Steam Engine, of 38 horse power, by Messrs Bates and Son, of Sowerby Bridge, and two Double flued Steam Boilers, of 40 horse power each, the Mill Gearing, Going Gear Shafts and Drums, and all other fixed machinery and things necessary to obtain the first motive power and to work and turn the Machinery in and about the said Mill and Buildings.
>
> The Site of the said Mill, Buildings Reservoir and Land, contains an area of 5 acres 0 roods 30 perches (more or less).

Martin & Sons Ltd

The mill and many extra pieces of land were bought by Patrick Martin and Joseph Liddell, with the help of a loan from the Halifax and Huddersfield Union Banking Company.[43] Housing for workers was eventually built on many of these plots of land.

The business could also take water from the 'drain' – not, as we might think, a channel for dirty water, but a freshwater stream that supplied the reservoirs of Wellington Mill and another mill in Oakes, owned by George Hattersley & Co.

Patrick Martin had come over from Ireland with his first wife, Sarah, and their children Ann and Henry. Settling initially in Kendal, the family retained links with that area for many years and maintained a holiday home there. The 1851 census suggests that both Patrick and Sarah came from that area, but this has not been substantiated.

The family later moved to Huddersfield, where baby Elizabeth was born in 1841. At that time they were living on Dock Street, right in the heart of town, and Patrick is described as a 'pattern drawer'.[44] He first worked for the firm of John Taylor & Sons of Newsome, but by 1849 he was earning sufficient to buy land – from George Lockwood of Dyke End, Huddersfield – at Laith Field[45] in Edgerton to build his own home, Ashfield House.

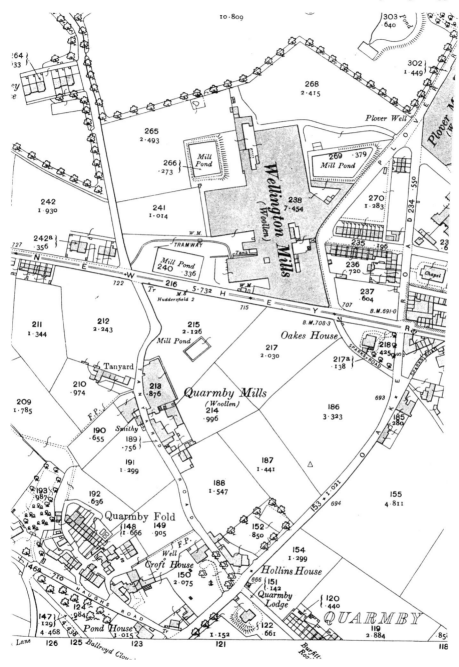

Ordnance Survey map 1907: scale 25″ to 1 mile.

White's 1853 Trade Directory shows him in Lockwood, still working as a pattern designer, but by 1859 he had joined the existing partnership of Liddell and Bennett, who had offices in Cloth Hall Street. This partnership was dissolved in 1864,[46] when Patrick Martin and Joseph Liddell bought the mill at Lindley. They began by making woollen cords which were then sold in the King's Head Yard. Not all was plain sailing, though.

In 1867 the firm were able to extend the buildings and built new warehousing. Whilst waiting for this to be completed, they stored 11,000lb (5,000kg) of wool in the teazing rooms. The combination of natural fibres and grease from the wool packed so closely together proved disastrous and the bales burst into flames. Even though the local police constable, PC Hawksby, smelt the smoke, roused the neighbourhood and quickly put out the fire, much of the wool was damaged and the fire had spread to finished pieces of cloth stored in the room above. The damage was estimated at over £1,200; only about £800 was actually insured so the firm had considerable losses.

A few months later, in September, the business was also in trouble in the courts. James Whareham, a weaver who lived in Oakes, Huddersfield, claimed £1 11s. 7d. (£1.58) for work done for the firm of Messrs Liddell and Martin. His lawyer stated

that he wove a piece for the defendants and when he brought it in on 17th August, they wanted to stop a certain amount for damages done to a piece woven in June. That piece, it was said, had been passed but he understood it was found afterwards to have been cut. If it had, it was cut after it left the weaver's hands and must have been done by the finishers.

The case was proved and Liddell & Martin had to pay the amount claimed, plus costs.

They continued there as partners for some time, appearing in the 1866 and 1868 directories as Liddell & Martin, woollen manufacturers at 9 Cloth Hall St and Wellington Mills. Later, Joseph Liddell left the business, sold his interest in the mills[47] and went into partnership with Sydney Herbert Brierley to form Liddell & Brierley of Stanley Mills, Marsh.

Martin continued at Lindley by forming a new partnership with William Edward Hirst and Matthew William Cliffe, but by 1875 this came to a natural end (most partnerships were for a set length of years). A notice appeared in the local paper[48] explaining that the new partnership would consist of Patrick Martin and Matthew William Cliffe, together with Patrick's sons Henry Albert and Edwin in co-partnership. Later his other sons joined the firm as well.

Workers' Treats
The practice of 'treating' the workers had been established early in factory life and Martins were no different. Though many mills simply put on a meal, there are records of various annual outings to the growing seaside resorts nearby and in June 1874[49] the workpeople were taken on a day's outing to Blackpool. The newspaper reported that

Accompanied by their wives and sweethearts, they left the Huddersfield Railway Station by special train at 5 am and arrived in Blackpool at 8.35. The first business on arriving was, of course, to get something to eat, having done which each followed his or her own bent, as to the manner in which they might amuse themselves. Some hired a stupid donkey which required a slatternly, rustic-looking lad to follow close to its heels, and to belabour it with a heavy stick in order to keep it toddling along; some visited the renowned Uncle Tom's Cabin; while others preferred a two hours' sail on the sea, which being rather turbulent, in consequence of the wind having got up considerably towards noon, no doubt caused many to contribute more to its contents than they would have done.

As well as annual works trips, special events were celebrated. On 13 February 1875 the workers were 'treated to a good substantial tea, laid out in one of the large rooms in the mill, tastefully decorated for the occasion which was to commemorate the marriage of Mr E Martin'. The workers drank the health of the happy couple and then dancing began 'to the inspiring strains of an efficient band'. There was also a glee party (singing group), composed entirely of hands at the mill. They sang 'Hail, Smiling Morn', 'Awake, Aeolian Lyre' and others. The evening ended with three cheers for the firm.

The workers responded by presenting Edwin Martin with a very valuable timepiece, a 'black marble clock, inlaid with malachite and enriched with engravings of gold.' On one side was an 'asteroid barometer' and on the other a calendar, surrounded by a chaste vase in green, bronze and gold. Joseph Sykes chaired the meeting and Joseph Calverley gave a speech. The clock was presented by Wright Firth, another cloth manufacturer in the area. These reports suggest a good relationship between workers and owners, at least part of the time.

Industrial Relations

Relations between boss and workers were not always so amicable. The textile industry suffered loss of markets in this period and, to alleviate the loss of profits, manufacturers tried to reduce wages.

On 8 February 1878, the local paper carried the story of a strike at Wellington Mills. A fortnight previously, the weavers had received notice of a reduction in the prices paid for weaving. The men refused to accept this. They offered to accept a small reduction on weaving plain cloth, but not on the fancy weaves, which were more difficult. The looms continued working for some time but, when agreement could not be reached, men began to walk out.

There were few associations that workers could turn to for help, but a strike in 1880 at Taylor & Littlewoods led to a Weavers' Association being set up, with an annual subscription of 4d. (2p). Further strikes followed at Martin & Sons. These led to the prosecution of some youths for picketing, which at that time was illegal.

The problem for many weavers was that their wage did not reflect simply their own ability and effort. It depended very much on the quality of the yarn they received and the quality of the loom they were working. If the loom broke, the weavers had to wait for loom tuners to come and mend it. Each employer paid their own rates, and the Huddersfield Woollen Manufacturers and Spinners Association was set up to try to fix uniform rates of pay. The rates the employers suggested would effectively have reduced pay for most workers, who were suspicious of any proposal by the manufacturers.

The men were on strike for over three months, despite the hardship this brought, since there was no strike pay or other support for their families. A meeting was called, attended by Edwin Martin and other employers as well as the workers, and reluctant agreement was reached on rates slightly modified from those offered by the employers.

Housing

Many workers lived fairly close to the mill, which is surrounded by terrace housing of two-up/two-down or back-to-back design, built before the turn of the last century. In contrast, Edwin Martin – described in 1881 as a 'woollen manufacturer employing 930 persons'[50] – was living in a villa in Edgerton. In 1884, he moved and the residence was advertised to let. It consisted of:

> Ground floor: entrance hall, dining room, drawing room, kitchen with scullery adjoining, nursery.
>
> First Floor: spacious bedroom with lavatory, wc separated from bath room, bedrooms over the drawing room.
>
> Two attic bedrooms
>
> Basement – keeping cellar, wash kitchen, coal place
>
> Coach house and two-stall stables. Garden and drying ground at back.

His elder brother, Henry Albert, later moved to the magnificent Stoneleigh, which eventually became a local authority home and is now divided into apartments.

Stoneleigh, the home of Sir Henry Martin.

The staff at Stoneleigh.

The house required a large staff to maintain it – a team of gardeners looked after the grounds, the greenhouses and fernery. The head gardener, Albert Crawshaw, worked there for many years until his death just before the First World War. Many girls were employed as maids and the children had their governess.

In contrast, the engineer at the factory, Richard Gee, had moved from the Halifax area into the Colne Valley and eventually to a terrace house on New Hey Road, within easy reach of the mill. The steam engines provided the only means of power: if

Worker housing on New Hey Road.

The Gee family. Back Row: Jane, George William, Richard. Front Row: Walker, Jinny, Lucy, Joe Edward.

anything went wrong with them, the whole mill could have lost production, so it was vital that the engineers could be called in quickly.

Often the job of engineer was passed on within the family, and that seems to have happened at Wellington Mills. Richard was the 'engine tentor', remaining in charge until his son, Joseph Edward, was old enough to take over. There was always more than one engine and they were often 'christened' with shiny brass nameplates.

The engines required constant attention and stoking, the massive boilers being in continuous use. At regular intervals, one boiler would be cooled down to allow for cleaning and maintenance. The huge leather straps on the engines needed constant checking and replacement.

This was very useful for the engineers, as their children never needed to go far for shoe leather. A descendant of one of the engineers told me that her dad would cut the required lengths from spare bits of engine straps, shape them and glue them to the offending shoes.

Brass nameplate from the Welli Mill engine.

A Second Generation of Martins

In 1881 Patrick, his second wife, Frances, and their son Fred spent some time at the Conishead Priory Hydropathic Establishment at Ulverston in Furness, Lancashire.

This was the Victorian equivalent of a health retreat, but it seems to have come too late for Patrick, who died the following year and was buried in the new cemetery at Edgerton where his first wife, Sarah, had been buried twenty years previously.

The business was soon exporting all over the world and an office was opened in London, which Horace Martin (Henry Albert's son) went to manage for a time. He then went on to manage the firm's interests in New Zealand. Travel and the opportunities it brought were important to the family. In 1903 Henry Albert, together with Edward Fisher JP, gave a large sum of money to establish a 'travelling scholarship' for students at the Technical College.

The recipients of the award were described as

Two in number, each of £70 a year, given for the promotion of commercial education. The holders to enter the service of a foreign firm for the year, and to report every six months to the Huddersfield Chamber of Commerce and to the Governors of the Technical College in the language of the country in which they are living at the time.[51]

The first recipient was Arthur E Swaine, but it does not appear to have been awarded again until 1906 when Harry Barwell, a cloth manufacturer, and Bernard Firth, studying chemistry, won.

The students had to go before a selection committee from the Chamber of Commerce. In July 1912, W A Bond, Herbert Brook, W P Clarke and J A Cockhill were interviewed, with the award going to W A Bond and H Brooke.

In July 1914 Alec S Firth, Ian M Todd and Hugh N Robie went for selection. Only one student, Alec Firth, is recorded as receiving the award that year, though a later note refers to:

The two students, who were holding Edward Fisher Travelling scholarships have been interned in Germany since the beginning of the war.

This led to the award being suspended until after the war.

In 1913 John Tinker put forward £1,000 for a similar award, favouring Spanish as the language to support because of the growing markets in South America, and the award became known as the Tinker-Fisher Travelling Scholarship. It is still awarded yearly by the Chamber of Commerce.

About the turn of the century, Huddersfield Corporation Passenger Tramway Dept began laying tramways, and included a stretch of track from the main line in New Hey Road to Wellington Mills at Oakes. Two coal chutes, numbers 39 and 40, at Hillhouse depot were rented by the mill from the railway company, and two coal trucks, each fitted with two 45hp traction motors, were specially designed and purchased by the corporation.

Coal was delivered directly to the mill via the main tramway system, being taken into a weighing area. The trucks were weighed as they came in full of coal, emptied and then weighed as they left, the difference being the amount of coal delivered.

In 1913 the firm gained the distinction of a visit from the king and queen. By this time it was 'the largest of its kind in the Huddersfield district' and the largest employer in the area, with 1,400 workpeople. There were a further 300 at Pellon Lane, Halifax, recently purchased, though there had been a branch there in 1884. The visit was a 'morale-booster' for the area, meant to thank them for all the hard work being put in producing cloth for the armed forces – and probably to encourage the workers to continue their efforts.

War and Changes

The First World War brought hardship for many, but the textile trade encountered boom years as their cloth was needed for army uniforms. The yarn used differed depending on the job. Most of the time the looms were weaving cloth destined for the infantry. No-one liked working on this because

the yarn was rough, poor quality and it often broke. We used to get really annoyed with it. But weaving cloth for the officers was different, they had much better quality! Even though we got a bit of a lower rate it was worth it not to have to work with that awful yarn supplied for soldiers' uniforms.

Martin, Sons & Co.
LIMITED
High-class Worsted and Woollen Manufacturers
HUDDERSFIELD ⌀ ⌀ Englanc

Specialities - Worsted Suitings, Black and Grey Coatings, Blue Serges, Dress Suitings, Trouserings, Overcoatings, etc.
TROPICAL SUITINGS FOR ALL CLIMATES.

This activity caused an increase in profits and the government was not slow to realise this. They brought in an Excess Profits Duty, payable on profits above the average pre-war amounts. Martin and Sons found their profits had increased by £100,000 in this time, but £80,000 went in taxes[52] though this still left the firm enjoying the benefit of £20,000 extra profit from the war.

After the war, depression gradually began to hit the industry again and trade unions expanded. Union leaders travelling from mill to mill, holding meetings during lunch hours outside

Letterheading of Martin & Sons Ltd.

FABRICANTS DE TISSUS DE LAINE PEIGNÉE ET DE LAINAGES DE QUALITÉ SUPÉRIEURE.
Spécialités :
Tissus de Laine Peignée pour Complets, Tissus Noirs et Gris pour Vestons, Serges Bleues, Etoffes pour Complets, Etoffes pour Pantalons, pour Pardessus, etc. Tissus Légers pour tous les climats.

FABRICANTES DE TEJIDOS DE ESTAMBRE Y DE LANA DE CLASE SUPERIOR.
Especialidades :
Tejidos de Estambre para Ternos, Negros y Grises para Gabanes, Sargas Azules, Tejidos para Ternos de Etiqueta, para Pantalones, Sobretodos, etc. Tejidos para Ternos para todos los Climas Tropicales.

MANIFATTURA DI LANERIE E STOFFE DI LANA PETTINATA SUPERIORE.
Specialità :
Stoffe di Lana Pettinata per Completi, Stoffe Nere e Grigie per Abiti, Saie Azzurre, Stoffe per Abiti di Società, Stoffe per Pantaloni, per Soprabiti, ecc. Stoffe per Completi Tropicali per Ogni e Qualunque Clima.

Фабриканты первоклассныхъ камвольныхъ и шерстяныхъ матерій.
Спеціальности : Камвольныя матеріи для мужскихъ костюмовъ. Черные и сѣрые матеріалы. Синія саржи. Матеріалы для вечернихъ костюмовъ. Брючные товары. Пальтовые матеріалы, и т.д.
Легкіе костюмные матеріалы для всѣхъ тропическихъ странъ.

the mills to try to increase membership. At Wellington Mills, the National Union of Textile Workers held several meetings outside the mill gates, before finally meeting at Oakes Working Men's Club at 5 pm on 5 December 1922.

The 'shop collector' (responsible for collecting subscriptions) for the menders was Annie Townend from Oakes. Each type of job had its own collector at Wellington Mills, since there were so many employees – Florrie Tinker for the burlers, A Dearnley for the finishers and C E Mitchell for the dyers. J W Haigh is listed first under the firm's name, so may have been the leader of the group.[53]

Pat Martin had started the business with only 20 looms, but by 1910 there were 235 looms running – increasing later to 600 looms[54] – and the mill covered $4\frac{1}{2}$ acres (2 hectares) of land, employing over 1,700 people in the area. The mill almost ended its life when a bomb hit it in 1940.

Sir Henry Martin.

The bomb did considerable damage, causing the evacuation of many in the area, but the buildings were repaired and business picked up again.

This revival was short-lived and the trade in textiles went into considerable decline. In 1958, on the brink of bankruptcy, the business was sold to the Tulketh Group. Henry A Martin resigned from the Board and the business lost its connection with the Martin family, though the name was retained and is still in use.

After reconstruction, the premises in Halifax were sold and production was moved to Brookfield Mills in Kirkheaton with just 150 employees, later transferring in 1976 to Kirkheaton Mills.

The Later Twentieth Century

W H Thomas, fine worsted manufacturers, took over part of the mills for some years. Then in 1960 John Gladstone & Co, a Scottish firm of cloth finishers, moved into the mills. Their managing director, D Finlay Maxwell, had studied at Huddersfield Technical College and worked for a time at John Crowther & Sons, so he was no stranger to Huddersfield.

He was also an electronics expert and introduced many new machines and processes to the business, including electronic scanning systems for 'straightness accuracy' for checks and plaids to conform to European standards. Gladstones also diversified into producing cloth for such items as loudspeakers, fabrics for pool tables and artificial crushed suede for wall coverings.[55]

Parts of the building were no longer safe to be left and in 1972 the 175ft-high (53m) chimney was pulled down.[56] The recently retired engineer, Joe Edward Gee, watched in dismay as his beloved engine-house was destroyed too, as the boiler-house had to be demolished to allow the chimney enough space to fall.

'He just sat on the seat at the top of the road and watched them. All day.' The chimney was described in the 1930s as 'one of the most beautifully designed mill chimneys to be found anywhere in the industrial north, as well as one of the best behaved in the district'[57] – meaning that it rarely belched out the obnoxious smoke that other chimneys seemed to suffer from. The coping stones around the top weighed over a ton each and had to be dropped down into the yard.

Gladstones seemed to be a thriving firm, which in 1981 was reported as having made extensive investment in new technology with a 'micro-processing department' and spending '£250,000 purely on research and new methods of dying [*sic*] both yarn and piece goods'.[58] But the decline in trade eventually hit the firm and in 1992 Gladstones closed, moving production to their Scottish branch, but retaining ownership of the buildings as 'investment property'.[59]

The mill owners tried hard to sell it for continued use. However, it was considered that 'The plant had one of the poorest layouts for a spinning mill ...' and no buyer was forthcoming. Planning permission is now being sought to transform the mill into accommodation – demolishing the old sheds at the rear of the five-storey mill building and building blocks of apartments instead, as well as converting the mill itself into apartments. The whole area is to be landscaped.[60]

Entrance with clock tower, Wellington Mills

Other Mills in the Area

Birkby township

Bay Hall Mill	Used mainly by Stork Bros, Angola yarn manufacturer; also D J Green and Charles Walton Ellis Ltd in 1910.
Clough House Mill	Demolished; site used by Asda supermarket; now housing.

Lindley cum Quarmby township

Acre Mill	Founded by John Sykes and developed by his widow, Charlotte, before becoming home to Sykes Bros Ltd, card makers, which became English Card Clothing. Recently bought by Huddersfield Royal Infirmary for redevelopment as office and nurses' accommodation.
Portland Mill	See main text above.
Wellington Mill	See main text above.
Oakes Mill	Built *c.*1820 for Ben Crosland & Sons; now industrial units (some textile use), for sale and future unknown.
Plover Mill	Joseph Walker & Sons established this mill in the early nineteenth century; at the end of the century, Smith & Calverley moved in and remained until replaced recently by English Card Clothing.
Quarmby Mill, Tanyard Avenue	This was in use by Henry Haigh & Sons from 1890 onwards, with Taylor Brothers, weavers, leasing part by 1910. It is now used by a stone merchant.
Temple Street Mill	Messrs Moore & Wilson suffered a fire here in 1877 but it seems there was little damage.[61] Alfred Crosland & Sons and Lindley Spinning Co were also in this mill. Now demolished.

Marsh township

Hollin's Mill	Also called Shaw's mill, as it housed John Shaw & Co in the 1860s. In 1867 Messrs J & B Walker 'gave up their weaving business' here and sold their machinery.[62] By 1901 R E Lumb was here with Edwin Sykes. Messrs Schofield & Smith took some of the mill and were still here in 1950.
Luck Lane Mills	Messrs John Shaw were here in mid-nineteenth century.[63]
Marsh Mill	Used by John Crosland in the 1840s. Messrs Wm Quarmby moved here in the 1890s. J Haywood & Sons operated from here for most of the twentieth century. It is now leased as industrial units.

Marsh Mill.

Providence Mill	Joseph Dyson, woollen manufacturer, was here in 1857. The mill was leased to many firms, but was apparently owned by G H Pontefract, who also manufactured here.
Stanley Mills	Built *c.*1880, the mill was used by Liddell & Brierley Ltd (see Wellington Mills) for over 50 years. Now demolished and the site used for flats.

Paddock township

Crescent Mill	Pape & Co were in this mill until their takeover by Martin & Sons of Wellington Mills (q.v.). They eventually moved to Kirkheaton. The mills were then used by William Lawton Ltd, yarn spinners.
Gledholt Mill	See main text above.
Granville Mill	Many firms were in this mill from the mid-nineteenth century onwards. It was offered for sale in 1853.[64] William Lawton, yarn spinners, were here in 1910.
Lumb Mills, Triangle	This mill was certainly in use at the start of the twentieth century when Westfield Cotton Co were there.
Mark Bottom Mills	In existence by the mid-nineteenth century, when it was occupied by William & Joseph Thornton. By 1900 Ephraim Wood & Sons, waste pullers, were here and remained for many years.
Millgate Mill	Built *c.*1850, the mill housed Messrs Lawton & Addy, woollen and Angola merchants, in 1881. William Lawton Ltd also leased it for a time.
Paddock Foot Mills	Built on site of an old fulling mill near the River Colne.
Paddock Mills	See Gledholt Mills in main text.
Pedley's Mill	See Gledholt Mills in main text.

Millgate Mill, Paddock.

Scammonden township

Firth House Mill	Occupied – together with Upper Firth House Mill – by George Wheelwright in 1910.
Scammonden Mill	This is the mill that never was! The first stones were laid in 1861, the Scammonden Commercial Cotton Spinning Co Ltd was formed, but the mill was never finished. In the end the site was sold off[65] and the stones removed.

Chapter Three
North-East of Huddersfield

Lane Mills and the Learoyds

Early maps of Huddersfield show few streets or roads with specific names. The main road seems to have been referred to simply as Lane and was an early home to industry and dyeworks. Sir John Ramsden's canal was eventually built nearby and this helped provide both transport and water for the mills.

One of the principal families involved in mills in this area was the Learoyds. They gave their name to a bridge over the canal, near what is now Hill House Lane, a small back alley called Learoyd's Row and to Learoyd Street, the only street that still bears their name in this area.

When George III died and his son the Prince Regent finally became king, one of his first acts was to try to divorce his wife, Caroline. By this time, she was extremely popular and he was definitely not, so there was a huge outcry about the treatment of the queen and eventually the divorce bill was dropped. All around the country, bonfires were built, fireworks illuminated the sky and there was much rejoicing.

In Huddersfield a sheep was donated and roasted at these celebrations, with the meat being distributed to the poor of the area. It was given by 'Mr Learoyd' though unfortunately the report doesn't specify which one of the family was in such a generous mood, but it shows that the family were already prominent members of the community.

The 1822 Trade Directory shows William Learoyd the elder, one of the pioneers of the textile trade in Huddersfield, established as a woollen cord and velveteen manufacturer on Canal Bridge in Huddersfield. During the 1830s William lived on 'Lane, Huddersfield' but by 1841 he was on Leeds Road. William was already a substantial property owner and became a trustee of the Huddersfield District Banking Company.

Two of his sons – James and William the younger – lived on Town Lane Fields. This may refer to the land and mill buildings that William had bought in 1830 from Charles Spivey, a druggist.[1] He was also in partnership with a Mr Hobson as a woollen manufacturer until this was dissolved in 1867.[2]

William Learoyd & Sons operated from this area for many years. William's son, Edward Learoyd, won a medal in Great Exhibition in 1851 for his cashmere merinos,

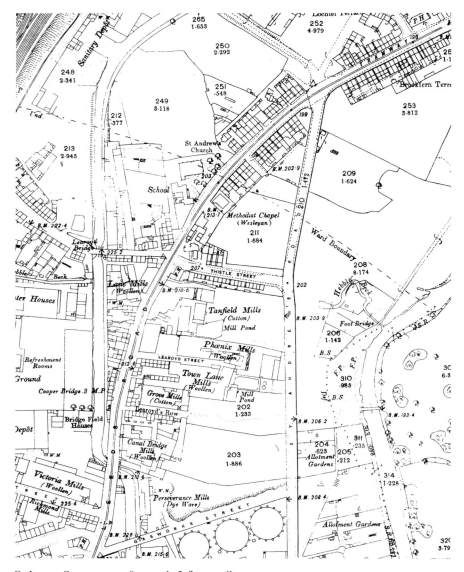

Ordnance Survey map 1893: scale 25″ to 1 mile.

which were used for the tops of ladies' boots, and for 'superior cloths' made of pure wool, with no recycled element, a policy retained by the firm.

It is possible that the mills were expanded or rebuilt about this time. A report of an accident in 1857 refers to 'Messrs Learoyd's new mill at Lane, Leeds Road'.[3] A stone mason called Thomas Mills, from Moldgreen, had been working on the building when a stone block fell on his leg, breaking it and requiring him to be taken to the Infirmary.

Early Strikes

As with all employers, there were times when industrial relations went awry. At the beginning of the nineteenth century, few were used to employing large numbers of people working together under one roof – nor were the workers used to these conditions. It was a steep learning curve for all concerned, but the workers were quick to realise that, if they stuck together, they might gain more than they could individually.

Many were used to obtaining some payment in advance for their work, but about 1855 the employers reduced this payment, making a difference of about 2s. (10p) per week in total wages. By 1857 this was causing considerable hardship to many weavers, who decided to strike to demand the payment's reinstatement.

In October 1857, weavers went on strike at Messrs Milner & Hale, Leeds Road, and at W Learoyd's, followed those at John Day & Sons, Moldgreen, and then at James Learoyd's factory. By Thursday morning, Edward Learoyd's workers were out. About 600 men and women joined the strike and the newspaper made the comment that 'It deserves to be recorded to the credit of those on strike that they have so far made no public demonstration, nor the slightest disturbances.'[4]

Just as nowadays, the two sides saw the problem differently. The employers wrote to the newspaper stating that the workers' pay on average was 8s. (40p), but could reach 10s. (50p), and that:

> The winders, who are girls from 13 years of age upwards, are paid from 5 to 6 shillings per week. The work of these young persons, beyond being necessarily on their feet, is not otherwise laborious.

The local weavers' committee disagreed. They considered the average wage was nearer 5s. (25p) and, even if a weaver could earn 8s.,

> is the figure sufficient for married women having a home to carry on and perhaps a child to put out to nurse, paying 2/- a week for the latter and 1/3d for the former and 9d for coals and taxes, leaving only 4/- to provide food and clothing at a time when potatoes are 15/- a pack and beef 9/- a stone. Is it a reasonable sum? Is it remuneration for their labour? Nay, is it a likely sum for a female without any encumbrance whatever?[5]

This does suggest that not all married women gave up work on marriage, or on having children, and that the need for child care is not just a modern phenomenon. It also suggests that, in the early days of unions, women were just as involved and just as likely to take action as men.

Out of this kind of dispute, which ended in compromise, grew unions and associations such as the Handloom Weavers' Protection Association, founded in 1872. When in 1874 their secretary, Mr Dyson, retired from the post, they presented him with a writing desk, a gold Albert (watch chain) and a purse 'for faithful and valuable service rendered as secretary in defence of the rights and interests of weavers generally'.[6] On thanking the group, Mr Dyson stated that he thought working life much improved!

James Learoyd & Sons

William Learoyd's son James began his own business in premises on Leeds Road, where the family had built Town Lane Mills and Tanfield Mills. James' sons, Charles, Albert and James, worked there for many years. In 1881 they were advertising for 'a good few menders' to come and work for them[7] but the firm of James Learoyd & Sons went bankrupt in 1891 owing almost £70,000 and the buildings had to be sold off.

Charles Learoyd does not seem to have played a high-profile part in town life, though he was a churchwarden and a member of the Conservative Club. One son, Charles Douglas, chose to follow a career in the army, becoming a major in the Royal Engineers. It was Charles' younger sons, Alfred Ernest and Frank, who carried on the family tradition, starting their working life at James Learoyd & Sons. They then set up their own business of Learoyd Brothers in Milnsbridge and later built Trafalgar Mills on Leeds Road.

Tanfield Mills

Learoyd's Land

William Learoyd the younger appears to have bought the land on which Tanfield Mills were built in 1843, as the transaction was referred to in a later Abstract of Title[8] when he paid £1,627.

In 1863 he and two of his sons, Samuel Turner and Robert, went into partnership in the mills as cloth manufacturers and yarn spinners, William taking a half share and each son having a quarter share. The value of the mills is given as £30,000, including the steam engines and stock. Further land was bought in 1877 to allow for expansion.

When William Learoyd and Sons left the mills in 1884, they put all the machinery up for sale by Auction:[9]

> From Tanfield Mills, Leeds Road, Modern machinery for the manufacture of woollen cloths:
>
> 11 condenser sets by John Haigh & Sons
> 5 pairs Mules by Knowles, Houghton & Co
> 60 ten quarter three-box power looms, 25 jacks by Hutchinson & Hollingworth
> Two willeys, two fearnoughts
> Two burring machines by John Sykes & Sons
> Dyeing, fulling, scouring & washing machines
> Whiteley's tentering machine and finishing plant
> Mechanics and smiths tools
> Mill furnishings and office furnishings

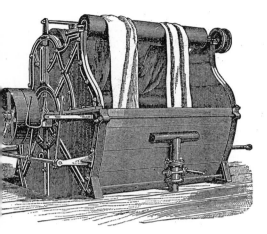

Early cloth-scouring machine.

All these machines are described as in good working order and no doubt continued in use for many years in other mills.

The mills themselves were also sold at the same time[10] by the local auctioneers, George Tinker & Sons. Lot 1 was the stone-built new mill, which was about 93ft long by 45ft wide (28 × 14m). It was four stories and an attic high, with external stone staircases and closets on the landings for each floor. The staircase was covered at the top with a large iron cistern.

Next to the mill was the beaming room and sale room, together with a 'lofty dyehouse' containing four stone cisterns, firing-place and boilerhouse, with a yarn store above. There were also a detached press shop, shoddy place and closets in this area.

In addition, there was the old mill, 89ft long by 41ft wide (27 × 12.5m) and four storeys and an attic high, with a stone staircase, engine-house covered with iron cistern, firing-place and boilerhouse, with store above. Behind the old mill was the willeying room, two storeys high with a tentering shed at the end, near the storage reservoir. Adjoining Leeds Road was the weaving shed with flagged floor and 'well lighted' – as all weaving sheds needed to be but often were not.

At that time there were two octagonal long chimneys with base course and moulded cornices. In the boilerhouse and steam room was a new steam boiler by Daniel Adamson, a second steam boiler and Green's economiser, as well as two condensing beam engines of 25 and 20 horsepower by R Gledhill and R Taylor and Sons.

The advertisement also tells us that the engines and shafts were so arranged that both mills could be worked from the engine in the new mill or the one in the old mill. Being able to keep both mills working whilst one engine was being repaired must have been an important selling point.

Another advantage for this mill was the well which, at 132yd (121m) deep, was said to contain 'a never-failing supply of water'.

William Whiteley's tentering machine for drying cloth.

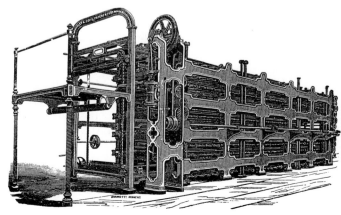

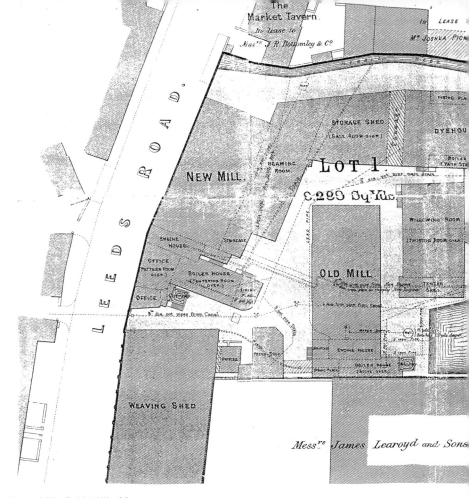

Plan of Tanfield Mill 1882.

This could be pumped into the cistern over the engine room in the old mill. The mills were also able to obtain an extra supply from the canal on the west side of Leeds Road, through pipes already laid.

The total area covered by the mill and its unoccupied ground was 8,288 sq. yd (6,930 sq. m) with a frontage to Leeds Road of 328ft (100m). Also to be sold was building land to the east, which fronted onto St Andrews Road.

Glendinning's

Tanfield Mills were bought by members of the Glendenning family, who were originally farmers in Scotland. As with many other families, when there were too many sons, some had to leave; so in the 1780s William and his brother Charles moved from Scotland to work in Bradley Mills, in the finishing department. William's son Alexander began working as a merchant in New North Road under the name of Alexander Glendinning & Sons, this business eventually being continued by Alexander's two sons, Charles and Alexander.

In 1874 Edward (another son of Alexander) and Charles began a partnership with John Beaumont as woollen manufacturers, but this seems not to have worked out as the partnership was dissolved by mutual consent early the following year[ii] and on 1 April 1875 the firm of Glendinning Brothers was formed. This included a fourth brother, John William.[12]

The firm of Beaumont and Glendinning began trading from Whitley Willows in Kirkheaton and were certainly there up to 1877 when they were paying rates to Kirkheaton District Council, but that year they moved to River Mill in Leeds Road.

They seem to have moved their machinery from Kirkheaton to River Mill in the same year, when the total was valued at over £1,000 and included power looms, twisting frames, burring machine and office furniture valued at £28. By 1886 the total value of machinery was almost £3,400. When they purchased Tanfield Mills in 1886, they must have also purchased the machinery too, as their Machinery Account shows an increase to over £6,400 in that year.

Under the Factory Act 1844 all firms had to have certificates signed by a doctor to confirm that the children they employed appeared to be thirteen years of age and were fit to work. Records of Beaumont & Glendinning show that Emma Jane Riches was one such who began work in 1873 in Whitley Willows Mill when she was just 13. She was seen and certified by Dr Greenwood as being of age and healthy.

Emma probably began as a piecener, twisting together broken yarn, before becoming a power-loom weaver herself. In 1878 she is shown as having material 'in the loom' in the company's stock inventory and by 1881 she gives her occupation as 'worsted weaver'. The ledger books show her 'work in the loom' listed as one of the assets of the company.

Her younger brother, Fred, passed his 'Standard Five' at school and was given his certificate from the headmaster, Henry Whiteley. Once he was examined by the surgeon, he began work at the mill as a woollen winder. Most families in

Extract from stock ledger, Beaumont & Glendinning.

the area all had the same occupation, as children usually followed their parents. In this case the parents had been in domestic service as cook and butler, but there was probably little opportunity in the small village for service.

Charles Glendinning

Like many other businessmen, Charles Glendinning took an active part in local politics. He was chairman of the town's Finance Committee, served on school boards and was a member of the council for twenty-five years (1873 to 1898). For fifteen years he was an alderman.

Nor was he averse to becoming involved in controversy. After the 1870 Education Act, the government had decided that, if it was contributing towards children's education, it should find out how the money was being spent. Some inspectors took a heavy-handed approach and were very much disliked. Charles Glendinning took the part of the teachers when one inspector had chastised a pupil teacher in front of the class. The newspapers carried considerable correspondence on the subject, mostly against the action of the inspector, commenting that he seemed to have no idea of what teaching was really about.[13]

Charles took an active part in meetings, though one suggestion did not go down too well. In 1883, Sunderland Council had allowed a prizegiving ceremony in their art gallery. When there was an announcement that children in the main hall would get their prizes first, the ones on the balcony promptly stampeded. Since someone had bolted one of the doors, 183 children died in the resulting crush and many others were injured.

Councillor Glendinning commented at the next Huddersfield meeting regarding previous discussions about entrances and exits from council buildings that 'like many other matters it appeared to have been consigned to the limbo of officialism, but perhaps in view of the terrible calamity which had recently taken place at Sunderland the matter might receive some consideration'.

He moved to express the town's condolences and also to vote 50 guineas to a compensation fund. The others on the council said there was no occasion for such a fund and anyway they couldn't vote on such a thing, so eventually the matter was dropped.[14] Another idea was more successful:

> Charles was the one who had the idea of having post boxes attached to the trams, so that all along the route people could post their letters which could then be brought back to Huddersfield for sorting.

He was not the only Glendinning involved in public life. His brother John William did much charity work for the Primitive Methodist church at Northumberland Street and was also a member of Huddersfield Naturalist and Photographic Society. All the family made regular contributions to local charities, including the Orphan Home and the cricket ground at Fartown.

Glendinning Brothers

By 1910 Glendinning Brothers had 120 looms in the mills, producing fancy worsteds and woollens and this level was maintained until after the First World War. During the war years, mills in the area turned to making uniforms, army blankets or other fabric needed by the government, and full employment became the norm.

It were hard work, but we stuck together – married women coming back into work waiting for news from t'Front, us young lads waiting to go; we all knew what we were weaving, our lads would soon be wearing and it made us think on, like.[15]

The firm was eventually taken over by Edward's three sons: George, who was managing director and mainly looked after the wool side of the business; Henry, who controlled the worsted side; and Ronald, who was responsible for the finances. When

Telegraphic Address :
"TANFIELD,
HUDDERSFIELD"
ABC Code,
5th Edition
Marconi International

London Office :
18 GOLDEN SQUARE
LONDON

GLENDINNING BROTHERS LTD.

Tanfield Mills, Leeds Road, Huddersfield, England

SPECIALITIES :
**Medium Fancy Worsteds and Woollens
Suitings and Trouserings
Vicunas, Serges and Overcoatings**
SPECIALITIES MANUFACTURED TO SUIT BUYERS' REQUIREMENTS

Orders executed direct by Cash Payment against Bill of Lading, or through the usual buying channels. Samples sent to responsible Buyers with reference. Please send copy of order when buying through Merchants.

Spécialités :
Tissus de Laine Peignée et Lainages Fantaisie de Qualité Moyenne. Tissus pour Complets et pour Pantalons. Vigognes, Serges et Tissus pour Pardessus.
Spécialités Fabriquées selon les Besoins des Clients.
Commandes exécutées directement contre payement au comptant contre connaissement ou par les intermédiaires habituels. Echantillons envoyés à tout acheteur établin muni de références. Prière de nous adresser duplicata de toute commande faite par l'entremise d'exportateurs.

Especialidades:
Tejidos de Estambre y de Lana Medianos, de Adorno, Tejidos para Ternos y Pantalones, Vicuñas, Sargas y Paños para Sobretodos.
Fabricamos artículos especiales para satisfacer las necesidades de los compradores.
Los pedidos se ejecutan directamente mediante pago al contado contra conocimientos de embarque o por los medios comerciales de costumbre. Se envían muestras a compradores de responsabilidad que den referencias. Al hacer pedidos por medio de comerciantes envíese copia de las notas de pedido.

Specialità :
Stoffe Medie Fantasia di Lana Pettinata e di Lana per Completi e per Pantaloni. Vigogne, Saie e Stoffe per Soprabiti.
Manifattura di Generi Speciali per Soddisfare e Fabbisogni dei Signori Compratori.
Si eseguiscono gli ordini direttamente per pagamento contanti contro Polizza di carico oppure per tramite delle solite vie d'acquisto. Si spediscono campioni a Compratori serii con riferenze. Si prega volér trasmettere copia dell'ordine passando delle ordinazioni per tramite di negozianti.

Letterheading of Glendinning Brothers Ltd.

George's son, Edward, took over in the 1930s he gradually reduced the amount of worsted and turned the mill primarily to wool.

Against the background of depression and the General Strike of 1926, the number of looms fell to 108, continuing at about this level for the next 30 years. The next major recession in the 1960s saw the number of looms drop to 85, before the firm finally went out of business in the 1970s.

However, before then the firm was responsible for some innovations in the textile industry. They were the first in Britain to produce foam-backed woven woollen fabrics.[16] Edward Glendinning had been on a trip to America, seen the fabric and decided not to wait until they flooded the UK market, but to get in there first. The material was warm yet lightweight and its use increased over the years.

The firm also 'invented' the instant skirt which was 'skirt material with a built-in elasticated waistband, leaving only the hem and one side to be attached by needle and thread' at half the price of buying similar material to make a skirt with fitted waistband. The fabric was titled 'Glenflex' and was made in a variety of patterns and cloths, tweeds, plains, pure wool and tartans.

They were extremely popular, being quick and easy to make up.[17] 'We could buy a length, get out the sewing machine and have a new skirt all ready to go out to the pictures that evening.'[18] This kind of 'instant skirt' can still be purchased in the Huddersfield area. Two years later, in 1966, they were producing a dress on a similar basis, this time with smocking at the waist.[19] Both these innovations were successful and exported to many countries.

Unlike many businesses, Glendinnings saw the writing on the wall and decided to go into voluntary liquidation whilst their assets would still cover their debts. The director cited the 'difficulty in making any profit in the present state of the UK home market' as the reason for this closure – the credit squeeze, high interest rates, slow payments from customers and increased unit costs had finally taken their toll.

New production stopped in July 1970 and the machinery and office furnishings were auctioned off in 800 lots in October of the same year. The buildings were sold to the builders' merchants Graham Gratrix. The mills and the 100ft-high (30m) tower were demolished in 1971.

Trafalgar Mills

Trafalgar Mills were built in 1896 to the specific design of Alfred Ernest Learoyd. Many mill owners had the problem that a multi-storey mill was not very efficient in

Ordnance Survey map 1893: scale 25″ to 1 mile.

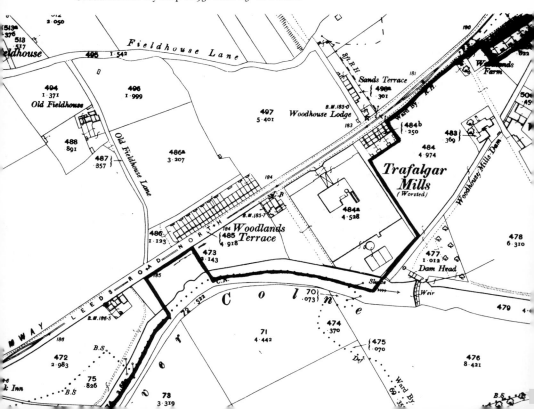

Plan of a revised, model mill.

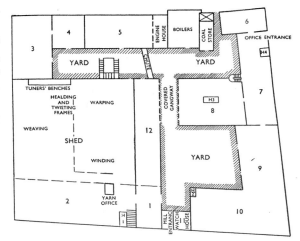

terms of organisation. Weaving was often done in more than one area, frequently in middle floors where the light was not good. Mending also tended to be done in any spare space, even though it too required excellent light if the menders were to do their job properly. Cloth was often transported back and forth across the mill yard from one process to another.

All these weaknesses in layout were discussed in a 1934 book by D R H Williams. With the aid of a numbered plan, he analysed the problems of one typical mill:

1. This building[20] was 3 storeys in height with most of the weaving being done in this area, often on the middle floors which had very poor light supply.
2. Although the top floor [which had good light] was used for weaving, the bottom floor was used for mending. Women would be hunched over lengths of cloth, desperately trying to see breaks in the thread, or untie knots and work them in. If mending was not done efficiently, the finished cloth would be of poorer quality.

The only workers with enough light were those next to a window on an external wall.

5. Scouring and milling were on the ground floor. These processes needed a good supply of water and the floor would often be awash with liquid. It made sense to house the processes here where a stone floor could be laid.
6. Pressing of the finished cloth was on the ground floor.
7. The warehouse was on the second floor, which meant that bales of finished goods had to be hauled up the hoists, and down again when they had to be delivered to the customer.
8. Tentering (stretching the cloth after washing) was on the ground floor, with finishing processes on the second floor.
9. Warping machines were on the middle floor which was quite dark. To alleviate this, a small glass light had been put in the floor above, but how workers managed to avoid falling through, or breaking the glass is a mystery. It also proved to be useless, since it merely collected dust and waste or fluff from the weaving which was carried out on the top floor. At least this did mean that the yarn only had to be transported up one floor to be used in this building.

10. Weaving was on the top floor, making use of the extra light from the windows which the architect had included, just in case the light might be useful.

Apart from poor light, a major cause of inefficiency was the poor arrangement of work areas for successive processes:

12. Healding was done on the top floor of this building. This necessitated the beams being taken from the second floor of building 9, to Hoist 1 near the yard entrance, up to the healding room then around the top floors of sections 1 and 2 or down the hoist to the shed or across to the top floors of 9 and 10.

Yarn was in boxes wherever there was space, and machinery was simply put in as it was bought with little forward planning.

Model Mills

The mills which the Learoyd brothers had worked in previously were arranged in a similar way. Bringing all the processes together was a relatively new idea and most mill owners were learning as they went along. But Alfred Ernest understood the process well, could see what needed doing and aimed to co-ordinate working so as to prevent loss of time and improve output to its maximum.

Trafalgar Mills spread out all on one storey, so that production was very efficient. It became a 'model' mill rather than the usual motley collection of buildings piled higgledy-piggledy around each other. The mill was built as a square. From the front entrance, the yarn went around the mill clockwise, visiting the various departments in the correct sequence, until it emerged as finished cloth at the right of the main entrance. Henry Ford may have imagined he invented the system, but a Yorkshireman got there first!

Trafalgar Mill.

Trafalgar Mills have always been considered among the best-looking mills in the area. Their ivy-clad frontage made the mills look more like an ancestral hall than a factory. The area surrounding it was landscaped with lawns, flower beds and trees. Learoyd's were one of the first employers to provide sports facilities for their workers with cricket pitches, a tennis court and bowling greens opposite the mill.[21] The ivy was eventually removed in 1973.

Alfred Ernest Learoyd was a member of the Huddersfield Fine Cloth Manufacturers association but he seems, like his cousin Charles, to have taken little active part in local politics. He was very interested in sport and was a founder member of the Huddersfield Golf Club. His only son, Geoffrey, died on active service in India in 1918 and later Alfred Ernest had a window installed in St Andrew's Church in memory of the late James and Elizabeth Learoyd.[22]

Huddersfield Fine Worsteds

In 1920 Learoyds amalgamated with Joseph Sykes & Co and A Crabtree & Co to form Huddersfield Fine Worsteds, with A E Learoyd as chairman. The new group went on to win two gold medals at an exhibition in Los Angeles.[23]

In 1948 the firm opened a branch at Fitzwilliam, near Pontefract,[24] where about 120 people were employed. This was an unusual move, since that area is not known for textiles, but Learoyds sent some of their burling and mending to the plant. The firm continued at Trafalgar Mills until the late 1970s when they moved to Kirkheaton Mills, becoming part of the Tulketh Group of companies.

The Huddersfield Fine Worsted group were one of the first companies to produce and promote the use of 'own group' labels, which indicated that the cloth had been woven in Huddersfield and was of 100% pure new wool, with no recycled wool, but few other companies seem to have done so at the time. Learoyd argued that the label was a symbol of excellence, instantly recognisable to customers. This is now widespread practice in marketing, but it originated in a Yorkshire mill. Other mill workers told me that 'Learoyd's were always considered the best – you had to be good to work there'.

Cloth badge of Learoyd & Co.

Many people were anxious to see how these 'model mills of the West Riding' worked, since they were specially designed for textile production. Even royalty arrived: George V and Queen Mary came in 1918; and in 1949 the then Princess Elizabeth and Duke of Edinburgh visited the mills to see how Yorkshire cloth was made. On these occasions all the workforce turned out to welcome the visitors and production efficiencies were relaxed for the day.

In 1964 an Australian television crew began filming at Trafalgar Mills to show their countrymen 'what happens to all that wool' and eight years later the BBC filmed part of their *Made in Britain* series at Learoyds.[25] Visitors came from around the world too, including from the growing Asian market.[26]

Finding something different to obtain publicity is always of interest to marketing managers and Learoyds were no exception. In 1964[27] they produced the world's most expensive cloth from the world's most expensive wool, which cost 550d. (£2 5s. 10d., now £2.29) per lb. It was bought in Australia, spun in Bradford, woven at Trafalgar Mills and then exhibited at the Junior Chamber of Commerce.

Later, suit lengths were given to customers 'drawn by lots'. One pattern was a bird's-eye black-and-white design with soft red overcheck whilst the other design, which was extremely difficult to manufacture, was a reverse twist double plain in blue.

But increased competition meant finding ways of cutting costs and that often meant moving all production under one roof. In 1979 the mills, which had housed Learoyds and Josiah France, were advertised for sale at £520,000 by the Illingworth Mooris group, of which Huddersfield Fine Worsteds Ltd was now part.

The two companies moved to Kirkheaton and are now under same roof as two others in the sub-group – Martin's and Broadhead & Graves Ltd.[28] As cloth production was phased out and the machinery removed, the firm admitted that 'the crisis in textiles is so severe that few firms are likely to take the plunge to secure the mills and ensure their continuity in the industry'.

For a while the mill did indeed stand empty but soon there were employment hopes as the mill was sold to H C Sleigh, an Australian company, who had a bicycle and toy assembly plant in Salendine Nook on the other side of Huddersfield. Trafalgar Mills, described as having 119,000 sq. ft (10,300 sq. m) of manufacturing or assembly space plus 18,000 sq. ft (1,670 sq. m) office space, they considered to be ideal for their purposes.[29] Yet again, though, in 1982 the buildings were sold, to the development group of Bevilaqua.

It is not only ancient mills that are a fire hazard. In 1994 the buildings were ablaze when 'flames and smoke ripped through the second floor'.[30] Such was the efficiency of the fire brigade that most of the building was saved. They worked both inside and outside the mill to put out the flames, though this time it was modern technology they were most concerned with rather than bales of wool. It was also modern technology that seemed to have caused the fire – an electrical fault was blamed.

Like many mills, Trafalgar always had a feeling of camaraderie, fostered as much as anything else by the social activities. In 1999, former workers at Trafalgar Mills began a campaign to have the buildings listed as they were concerned at how many mills had been destroyed. The owners agreed that the front section of the building was worth listing, but not the warehouses at the back. Most have now been demolished and the buildings are in use as industrial units.

Other Mills in the Area

Bradley township

Holme Mill   Plans of a mill from 1872 show Mellor Brothers, cotton spinners, who remained here into the twentieth century.

Deighton township

Whitacre Mill	See Woodhouse Mill.
Woodhouse Mill	The mill here, built at the end of the eighteenth century and occupied by John Whitacre, was replaced in 1843. James Akroyd, cotton spinner, moved here *c.*1910 and the firm of William Thompson was here by 1914. Both were still at the mill in 1950, with John Lee Walker & Sons.

Huddersfield township

Albany Mill	See Gladstone Mill.
Albany Mill, Firth Street	Used by Allan Mallinson & Co in the 1890s, and by Albany Mills Co Ltd by the early 1900s.
Albert Ware Mills	Just off Lower Head Row near the canal, these mills may have been primarily a warehouse.
Albion Mill	Joshua Whiteley & Co Ltd occupied this mill from the 1850s for at least 100 years.
Ashbrow Mill	Brierley Bros were here before moving to Albert Mills, Lockwood (q.v.). H Lister & Co Ltd used the mill, until it was taken over by Crowther & Nicholson, who still use it.
Aspley – Lower	Greenwood Brothers were in this mill in 1852 when they took their workers for 'a substantial supper and coffee'.[31]
Aspley – Upper	James Mitchell had his works here, but went out of business in 1852.[32] Part of the mill was then taken by Charles Kaye,

Ashbrow Mill.

Britannia Mill, Huddersfield.

	cotton warp manufacturer, whose boiler exploded killing nine people in 1857.[33] John Eccles & Co used the mill in the early twentieth century but all the Aspley Mills are now being converted to flats.
Aspley Mills	This is a very old fulling mill, certainly there by the 1780s when Richard Atkinson held it, but many firms rented space over the years. Now student accommodation.
Britannia Mill, Colne Road	Built about the 1860s when J Hopkinson & Co were in it. Leased to many different textile firms including Joseph Lumb & Sons in 1910. Now used by Kirklees Council.
Canal Bridge Mill, Leeds Road	Occupied by George Brier & Co; described as woollen mill on 1893 map.
Chapel Hill Mill	Factory Commission report of 1816 shows this was Fisher's Silk Factory; later used by Kenworthy, Royston & Crossley.
Colne Bridge Mill	In the 1800s this was Pilkington land – in 1818 there was a disastrous fire, which killed seventeen young girls who had been locked in the mill. The 1834 Factory Commission Report [hereafter FCR 1834] shows Thomas Haigh & Sons, cotton carding and spinning. They remained associated with the mill until the early twentieth century.
Colne Road Mill	Built c.1855 by John Taylor & Sons of Newsome.

Commercial Mill, Firth Street	This was built in 1864 according to the datestone. J Schofield & Sons were there until *c*.1890; C Greenwood & Co into the twentieth century; now being converted into student flats.
Deighton Mill	Currently used by Barntex Ltd, textile merchants; Carrie & Benison were in this mill in 1910.
Eagle Mill, Lower Head Row	Shown on an 1893 map, near the canal.
Eastwood's Mill	See Engine Bridge Mill.
Engine Bridge Mill	This was a dyehouse and fulling mill by the beginning of the eighteenth century. By the 1830s, John Eastwood & Sons were making cloth here. The firm continued as Fred Eastwood & Co right into the twentieth century.
Fairfield Mill	Built in 1854 according to the datestone, it housed Cockroft & Lumb, which developed into Messrs Cockroft & Co by the end of the nineteenth century. William Hollins & Co Ltd were there for a time, now Yorkshire Fur Fabrics.
Fern Street Mill	Few references to this mill except that had a fire in 1908. Swallow Bros were in the mill in 1910.
Field Mill, Leeds Road	A later mill: Fred Carter & Co were there in 1874. Messrs Edwin Walker & Co moved there *c*.1880 and remained there for at least 70 years.
Firth Street Mill	A later mill, built *c*.1865 as a single five-storey building. Others were added as required. It was a cotton mill of Reuben Hirst & Sons in 1892. Now flats.
Folly Hall Mill	Built by Joseph Kaye in 1825, it was leased to many different firms over the years. In 1844 it suffered a fire but was rebuilt on a larger scale. At the time over thirty small businesses rented rooms in the building.[24] Joseph Lumb & Sons used the

Folly Hall Mill.

mill from 1900 onwards.[35] Some parts have now been demolished and the rest is empty awaiting a decision on its future use.

Gladstone Mill, Firth Street
Also called Albany Mill, this was built in the 1860s by John Eastwood of Meltham, but suffered severe damage in 1882.[36] The name was changed *c.*1890 because of the owner's changed political allegiance.

Grove Mill, Leeds Road
Associated with the family of Learoyd & Sons (see Trafalgar Mills), this was a cotton mill in 1893; J Firth & Sons were here up to the mid-twentieth century; now divided into industrial units.

Kaye's Factory
See Folly Hall Mill.

Larchfield Mill
A five-storey mill, it was built in 1865 by George Brook, who used it until *c.*1900. Shaw Brothers Ltd had this mill for the first half of the twentieth century, letting rooms to Richard Mellor & Co and others. Now converted for use by the University of Huddersfield.

Lane Mills
See main text above.

Lockwood's Mills
See Upperhead Row Mills.

Longroyd Bridge Mills
Also known as Starkey's Factory or Springdale Mills, this was built *c.*1819, on an island between the River Colne and the Huddersfield Canal, by Starkey Brothers, who also let rooms to other firms. By the start of Victoria's reign there were four mills on the site. In 1848[37] John Radcliffe, mason, and his men were pulling down old buildings at the woollen mills of Starkey Brothers, Longroyd Bridge. They found a purse of 294 sovereigns, eventually given to Huddersfield Infirmary. Ramsden & Co and Crowther & Vickerman Ltd leased part of this mill in 1910. Now demolished.

Longroyd Bridge Silk Mill
This appears to have been owned by the Starkey group, but was further along Thornton Road from their main mills. It was occupied by Edward Fisher & Co as a silk mill from c.1830. It is sometimes referred to as Fisher's Factory.

Manor Mill, Kings Mill Lane
Hobson & Son were in this mill.[38]

Mulberry Mills
These were in Fitzwilliam Street, though not shown on the 1906 map. William White, silk throwster, was in this mill after the Second World War.

Phoenix Mills
Blamires Ltd were woollen manufacturers here from the 1870s up to the 1960s.

Pioneer Mill, Fountain Street
Mentioned in 1950 as being occupied by Benjamin Thornton & Son.

Priest Royd Mill
This bears a datestone of 1869. It was used by John Haigh & Sons, who were machinists, not wool manufacturers. In 1910

Charles Lockwood & Sons were in the mill but the following year there was a massive fire. It has now been converted into flats.

Richmond Mill, Fitzwilliam Street John Sutcliffe & Sons, shoddy & mungo merchants, were in this mill from *c.*1880 into the twentieth century.

River Mill, Leeds Road Used by Glendinning Brothers in the 1870s, until their move to Tanfield Mills (q.v.).

Riverside Mills, Firth Street This was leased to many different businesses – Eccles & Watson Ltd, Millman, Hunt & Co and Jonas Horsfall & Sons are all shown there in 1950.

Seed Hill Mills A central mill near the canal at Aspley, it included a dyeworks.

Springdale Mill See Longroyd Bridge Mill.

Starkey's Mill See Longroyd Bridge Mill.

Tanfield Mill See main text above.

Town Lane Mills See main text above.

Tower Mill Built at Turnbridge, near the canal, the firm of J M Hassell was in the mill in the 1870s and A Laycock & Sons by beginning of twentieth century.

Trafalgar Mill See main text above.

Turnbridge Mill Built about the 1850s, this was leased by a number of firms before being taken over by J L Brierley, yarn spinners, part of the Brierley family from Saddleworth. They went on to form Rhodes & Brierley at Kirkheaton and Brierley Brothers at Lockwood (q.v.). It is still in the same family.

Upperhead Row Mills This six-storey mill right in the centre of Huddersfield suffered a severe fire in 1828[39] when it collapsed at a loss of £10,000. The buildings were uninsured, but Joshua Lockwood seems to have rebuilt them. Josiah Lockwood established his cord and velveteen manufactory here, eventually taking in a partner to become Messrs Lockwood & Keighley. The mill was destroyed in a fire in 1914 and the firm moved to Gledholt Mills (q.v.).

Turnbridge Mill.

Victoria Mills, Beaumont Street	Little is known about the origins of this mill, but it was built *c.*1890. Thomas Canby, cloth finisher, operated from this mill from 1910. John Sutcliffe, in shoddy and mungo, was in the mill in 1950, as well as at Richmond Mills.
Water Royd Mill	A mid-nineteenth-century mill near the canal at Turnbridge, this was occupied up to 1910 by Joseph Raynor & Co Ltd, woollen and Angola yarn spinners.
Waterloo Mill, Leeds Road	This was leased to various firms, including Butterworth & Sons, who were there c.1850 and still listed in 1910.
Wells Mills, Northgate	Built *c.*1830, this was a central mill, behind the wholesale market area, leased to many different firms, including Henry Brook & Sons and Rowland Hall, later of Portland Mill (q.v.). In 1910 it housed G H Fox & Co.
Wentworth Mills, Fitzwilliam Street	Rennards & Garside Ltd were here for the first half of the twentieth century.
Wharf Mills, Shorehead	There is a reference to Nelson Weaving Co Ltd at this mill in 1950.
Zetland Mill	Built in the 1850s by W H Ashton, who remained here for fifty years, it was also let to various firms including Walter Sykes Ltd, woollen and worsted manufacturers, who were there up to the Second World War.

Chapter Four
South–East of Huddersfield

To the south-east there were coal measures, which could supply fuel for steam power, though the early fulling and scribbling mills were on the Fenay Beck, which runs into the River Colne. This small waterway often dried up in the summer, so the mills needed an alternative form of power.

Some of the land in this area is suitable for arable farming or dairy cattle, as well as sheep farming, and many mill owners began as farmers as well as clothiers, gradually building up their businesses as the Industrial Revolution got under way.

View across the Fenay Beck landscape.

Bankfield Mill

John Day & Sons

Leaving Huddersfield to the south-east was the Austerlands Turnpike, leading to Wakefield and ultimately London. Almondbury had originally been the more important settlement in the area but, as the roads had improved and water power became needed for the mills, the small village of Huddersfield – close to the River Colne, the Fenay Beck and the River Calder – expanded, becoming the major market town.

Just on the outskirts of the town, as the road begins to rise up the hillside towards Almondbury, Bankfield Mills were built *c.*1829 by John, Thomas and Samuel Shaw and sold to Beaumont Taylor, a fancy-cloth manufacturer who needed the help of a mortgage from Benjamin Haigh Allen of Greenhead (who was also responsible for building Trinity Church at a cost of £12,000), Joseph Armitage of Milnsbridge and Joseph Walker of Lascelles Hall, to complete the purchase.[1]

In 1848 Beaumont Taylor and the firm of John Day & Sons were victims of the weather when 'terrific storms of thunder and lightning' devastated parts of Huddersfield. Moldgreen was one of the worst-hit places, being on a bank, and the floods poured down the hillside, causing damage and death. It was reported that:

Ordnance Survey map 1907: scale 25″ to 1 mile.

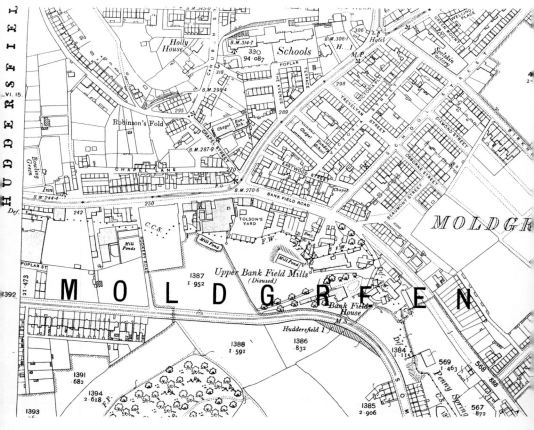

Bankfield Mill.

The new mill of Messrs John Day & Sons, a little higher up the hill and immediately adjoining Rookery Mill, was flooded more than three feet deep with water on the first floor from which the proprietors are serious sufferers. The dyehouse of Mr Beaumont Taylor, a short distance up Almondbury bank was likewise flooded and great injury done. A wall which ran parallel with the dyehouse but a considerable elevation above it about forty yards long coped with iron palisading, was torn down with the rush of water on the road, for about twenty five yards.[2]

John Day originally had his business in mills at Storths, lower down and nearer the Wakefield Road; he appears in White's 1837 Trade Directory of the West Riding as a Manufacturer of Fancy goods at 'Mould Green'. The Storths Mill had been a spinning mill and finishing shop, with store and dyehouse, warehouse and stables. Day also leased two houses on the site. The mill, in common with most older mills, was long and narrow, being 43 yards long and 7 yards wide (39×6.4m), three storeys high, with an 8hp steam engine, and lit by gas.[3]

When, in 1849, the larger premises of Bankfield Mills were advertised for sale, they were purchased by John Day and John Day the younger of Mold Green.[4] The new mill was stone-built and had a large warehouse behind the main house. The industrial buildings consisted of a two-storey, stone-built drying store of 45yd long by 17ft wide (41×5m), with a stone-built mill 20yd long, 11yd broad (18×10m) and four storeys high, plus an attic. Although it was shorter than his previous mill, it was wider and had extra floors. The firm also purchased the 15hp steam engine and two boilers, with boiler-house and drying-house.

On the north side of the mill were a weaving shed, 17 × 5yd (15 × 4.6m), a dyehouse of 27 × 7yd (25 × 6.4m) adjoining the mill, and a warehouse for dye stores. These had to be kept well away from the finished pieces of cloth to avoid damage. There was also a press shop on the ground floor and a pattern room on the upper floor, with a singeing house near the press shop. Since much of land had originally been farmland, there were also a stable for two horses, a mistal for four cows and a fold yard.

At its west end, the mill had a dam holding back a large reservoir, and there was a tank in the paddock above the premises.[5] The advertisement specifically mentions its 'never failing spring of excellent water', which was part of the secret of the firm's success.

Along with the mill, the Days bought Bankfield House – together with its 'pleasure gardens'. The sale price is not known but the ground rent (payable to the Ramsden estate, who owned most of the land in the Huddersfield area) was £23 5s. 2d. (£23.26).

An insurance policy with Leeds & York Fire Office valued the mill in 1850 at £2,500, which must reflect the actual purchase price the year before.

Presumably, it was because the floods in 1848 caused so much damage that it was another two years before the firm were able to hold a party for their workers. On the Monday evening of 16 February 1850, over 100 of the workforce sat down to a dinner of roast beef and plum pudding 'to celebrate their removal from the Storth, Mold Green to Bankfield Mills, lately purchased by the firm from Mr Beaumont Taylor'.[6]

As was usually the case, the dinner included many toasts to the queen and to their employers, and the party lasted until eleven at night; but, naturally, all the workers were expected to be back at work early the next morning.

The Day family had lived in Huddersfield for many years, rising from small beginnings to become substantial mill owners. At the time of moving to Bankfield, the family were living in Berry Brow, even the sons. Unusually for the time, both Joshua and William are simply described as 'at home'. This description is usually reserved for women who had no paid occupation.

The father, John, was not well, but the firm was ably run

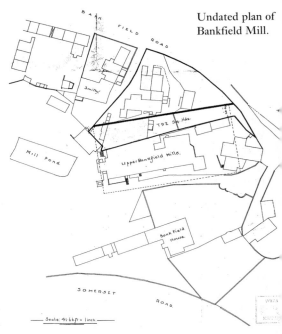

Undated plan of Bankfield Mill.

by two of his sons – John and William. The firm showed off their wares in the 1851 Great Exhibition at Crystal Palace. Although they didn't win any prizes, their products are described as:

> Merinos (cotton chain shot with woollen) used chiefly for the tops of ladies' boots. Cashmerettes, cotton shot with woollens and silk shot with woollens, used for summer overcoats.[7]

Whilst the textile industry in the West Riding is traditionally associated with wool, many firms used a mixture of fibres. 'Merinos' used wool from the merino sheep, mostly from Australia, but Day was also using some cotton yarn and silk. Although cashmere hair from the Himalayan goat was sometimes used, it was expensive and the 'cashmerettes' referred to were probably made of wool specially treated to look like the real Cashmere.

Hazards

Fire was an ever-present hazard in mills and Bankfield was no exception. On the night of 2 February 1867, it was reported that a fire broke out in the teasing room. Immediately the man working on the machine raised the alarm and a large number of hands rushed out with cans, buckets and any other vessel. Fortunately, they had a plentiful supply of water from the mill reservoir nearby, so the fire was quickly extinguished.

The damage was only a few pounds' worth and that was covered by the Royal Insurance Office so there was no great loss to the business. In this case it was decided that some hard substance had got into the cotton and, in the process of teasing, had come into contact with the teeth of the machine and ignited the flammable material. The incident shows that, even at this time, the mill was working both day and night.

It was, of course, in the interests of the mill hands to put out the fire as soon as possible. If the damage caused the mill to close, even for a short time, the workers would be laid off and receive no pay.

Like all mills, Bankfield needed its workers to be able to travel to and from their workplace. The Huddersfield tram service to Moldgreen began in 1885 but, for the first few years, the trams were horse-drawn. The half-hourly service took just over ten minutes, and the trams could carry up to 34 people.

It must have been difficult for the horses to pull such a weight up the hill. From 1888 the trams became steam-powered and, by 1902, electric-powered. The advent of electricity required the Huddersfield Corporation to negotiate with the mill owners for permission to place a rosette for the cables on the mill. The corporation paid one shilling annually for this privilege.

Local Involvement

The firm also took an interest in the Mechanics' Institute, paying membership subscriptions from the mid-nineteenth century onwards. Donations were also made to the building fund: £20 in 1858 and £100 in 1878.

Life changed in Huddersfield when it became a borough, with an elected council. John Day jr was elected to represent the Moldgreen Ward. Such was his standing that he was elected an alderman at the first meeting on 7 September 1868. John Day was also chairman of the Moldgreen Local Board, which took responsibility for local government and services in the area.

No doubt it was usually effective, but it failed to meet its obligations with regard to the road near to Kirkheaton church. Joseph Sheard, a coal proprietor, had complained about the roads and Moldgreen Local Board was summoned before the magistrates to account for its lack of action. The case was adjourned for one month to give the board time to repair the road, but, on 16 February 1868, the *Huddersfield Chronicle* reports that the board was fined 16/- (78p) for not having completed the road repairs.

A year earlier, in January 1867, at a meeting of the Local Board, Moldgreen, where John Day as Chairman presided, the matter for discussion was the proposed new roads to be created from Almondbury to Huddersfield. These would require six current footpaths to be 'stopped up'. There was much discussion about this, most of those present expressing the view that the new roads would open up land for building and increase the value of the land in the area.

Many of those present would have been the owners of that land, so the objection from 'Mr Mitchell, a working man' – that this would mean the way would be longer, particularly for those on foot – was over-ruled and the new roads were agreed.

In 1879, John Day & Sons leased further land and buildings in this area from the main Huddersfield landlord – the Ramsden Estate.[8] But in 1882, John Day decided to go with some friends on a grouse shoot. He had a slight cold before he went, and suffered a slight injury on the journey up to the moors when the pony trap he was in overturned. He had to be accompanied home by his brother, but bronchitis set in and within a few days he was dead.

His obituary[9] lists all his many activities for the borough, including being on the committees of Wormald's and Nettleton's charities, and the Chamber of Commerce. He had also been Vice-President of the Huddersfield Conservative Association and on the Board of Directors of the Infirmary as well as a Director of the Huddersfield and Upper Agbriggg Savings Bank.

Despite this setback, the firm continued to prosper. On John Day jr's death, his share in the business passed to his son, John William.

John Day jr's younger brother, William, also took an active part in local events. He was a Guardian of the Poor between 1878 and 1894, spent six years on the Huddersfield Town Council as ward representative, became in 1877 a director of the Huddersfield and Upper Agbrigg Savings Bank and in 1887 a director of the West Riding Bank as well. He was also involved with the Huddersfield Choral Society, Conservative Club and Christ Church in Moldgreen. On moving to Honley, he continued his activities with Farnley Tyas Local Board and Honley Urban District Council.

Joshua had been less active in the firm but family involvement continued through the interest of William's sons, Joshua and Albert Victor, and the sons of Samuel Day

– Thomas Horton and John. Albert Victor Day was another member of the family who was prepared to get involved with local affairs, serving as manager of the school in Moldgreen and as governor at the Technical College.[10]

W T Johnson & Co

By the beginning of the twentieth century, the house and mills were sold[11] for £3,700 to James Sykes of Huddersfield, who later sold them to Walter Thomas Johnson.

According to census returns, Walter Thomas Johnson was born in Whitby about 1861, though why the family had moved to that area is unknown. His mother came from Halifax, and his younger sister was born there in 1869. Just after this, his mother remarried and moved to Huddersfield, living in Cowcliffe, near Fartown.

Walter went on to work at Glendinnings' mills on Leeds Road as a Foreman Cloth Finisher. In 1916 the mill buildings were sold by Mr Sykes to Walter Thomas Johnson, but it seems he had been in business at Bankfield Mill for some years, since the firm of W T Johnson appears with that address in the Yorkshire Textile Directory for 1910 as 'dyers and finishers', telephone number Huddersfield 1588.

The eldest son, Walter Marshall, had originally planned to go into the civil service, and passed his exams to do so, but preferred to go into business with his father where Walter Thomas' practical experience combined with Walter Marshall's commercial studies to make a good team. Later, the other sons, Tom and Frank, became part of the family business. This tradition of family involvement has continued to the present day.

The firm specialised in finishing cloth to a high standard. Basic finishing involves washing, drying and pressing fabric from the weaving loom to produce fabric ready

Loom dated about 1930.

for the garment maker. There are many variations and additions to these basics to produce different finishes for different types of fabric.

For example, flannel fabrics are milled (pounding the fabric in warm soapy water to felt the fibres together), usually followed by brushing or raising to create surface effects. Other materials, such as crepes and tropical-weight fabrics, are washed very carefully so as not to disturb the surface, to give a clear, clean appearance.

Nowadays, additional chemical treatments are given to add qualities such as waterproofing, crease resistance, anti-static or flame resistance. As competitors in low-cost countries have been able to undercut UK manufacturers, the firm has specialised more and more in very high-value wool fabrics, often blended with other expensive fibres such as cashmere silk and mohair.

Part of this finishing requires a constant supply of clean water. By the 1930s, all knowledge of the original supply to the site seems to have been lost, so drilling experts Thomas Matthews were brought in to find a supply for Johnsons. Whilst wells are normally only about 300ft (90m) deep, the firm had to drill for 1,500ft (457m) before finding the water needed. As the firm's booklet states: 'from that time the firm has reaped the benefit of its own uncontaminated free water-supply.'

The firm continued to expand and in the 1950s was able to buy further land from the council for development. This is the site in operation today – and not only is the mill still a textile mill, but it is still owned by the same family. However, they do not just look to the past.

Operations have been fully modernised, with due regard to the environment. As they say, 'we still use soap for washing our fabric, whereas almost all companies world-wide have replaced soap with detergents, and this gives the company a leading edge in today's marketing climate where 'natural' and 'sustainable' are coveted buzzwords'.

The firm has continued to look for new technology to sustain their growth. In 1977 they installed an Ekofast continuous finishing machine, which combined blowing, high-temperature setting and pressing in one continuous process. These are normally three separate processes.

This proved so successful that a second Ekofast machine was installed 10 years later and these are now the only two such machines in the western world. The machines also added an additional quality control factor of weft straightening.[12]

A further investment caused the road outside their mill to be closed off on a quiet Sunday morning in 1980 as a 35ft-high (10.7m) bulk storage silo was delivered and installed. It is used for dissolving the light soda ash used in the textile finishing process and it represented a considerable investment programme for the firm.[13] W T Johnson & Sons remain confident in their ability to stay ahead of the field in the future.[14]

Dearneside Mills

Jonas Kenyon moved to Dearneside from Cumberworth in the 1850s, at first to premises at Bank Lane, Denby Dale. A partnership of Jonas and three of his five sons, John, William Henry and Arthy, was formed in 1880 and they moved to Dearnside in 1883.

Business Relations

The firm traded with both local and national businesses. Glazed papers were bought from Thomas Sykes of Golcar at 3¼d. (1⅓ p) per lb. Henry Crossley of Holmfirth supplied shuttles and screws, whilst E Milner supplied bobbins by the gross. More machines needed to be purchased in 1884. A secondhand tentering machine came from W Whiteley & Sons of Lockwood, whilst further quotes were obtained from Kenworthy, Royston & Crossley of Huddersfield for finishing machinery.

Many businesses worked on commission, dyeing, spinning and weaving for other textile firms. Among other firms, Kenyons wove cloth for Ehrenbach, Braun & Co of Bradford according to their own designs, whilst yarn was put out to be dyed at Thomas Brierley & Sons of

Jonas Kenyon (1817–1890).

Denby Dale, Cartwright & Co of Thurlstone near Penistone and David Lockwood at Kirkburton – all within easy reach of the mill at Dearneside.

During 1881–2, Kenyons used the local firm of James Littlewoods in Denby Dale. Their invoices show a range of colours – indigo blue, black, scarlet, green, blue, magenta, violet and primula. But business relations were not always cordial.[15] In 1884, Messrs Thomas Brierley of Denby Dale wrote, saying:

Gentlemen

Yours of the 4th is now before me, and is such, I suppose as you have been accustomed to with Messrs Littlewood. Allow me to tell you it is at all times a great pleasure to us to oblige our customers 'great or small' but certainly object to be dictated to by you and in such a manner as you think fit. We existed a long time since without your assistance or insults and can do again.

Yours

John Brierley

Letterheading of J Kenyon & Sons.

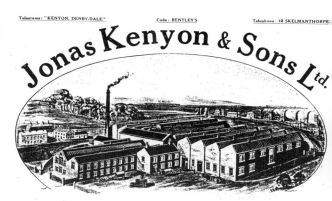

Telegrams: "KENYON, DENBY-DALE."   Code: BENTLEY'S   Telephone · 12 SKELMANTHORPE

Jonas Kenyon & Sons Ltd.

All Communications to be addressed to

Dearneside Mills,

DENBY DALE,

HUDDERSFIELD, 15 EXCHANGE.

Nr. Huddersfield, England.

High=class Worsted Manufacturers

Worsted Tennis Cloths and Gabardines, Indigo Serges in all weights. Dress Coatings, Trouserings, Fancy Vestings, Brocades for Shoes.

Orders executed direct by Cash Payment against Bill of Lading, or through the usual buying channels.

Fabricants de peignés supérieurs.	Manifattura superiore di Lana da pettine.	Fabricantes de tejidos de estambre de clase superior.	本廠專織高等羊毛毛足
Draps tennis et gabardines en laine peignée, serges indigo en tous poids. Étoffes pour habits, pantalons, vestes fantaisie, brocarts pour chaussures.	Panni e Gavardine di lana da pettine per Tennis, Sale indaco in tutti i pesi. Stoffe per abiti di società, per Pantaloni, Panciotti fantasia, Broccati per calzature.	Tejidos de estambre para tennis y gabardinas; sargas azul añil de todos pesos. Tejidos para gabanes de vestir, pantalones, chalecos de adorno, y brocados para zapatos.	打球服裝用布惹色, 薄絨布料外套用布, 裌袄用布神絲製雜用布
Les commandes sont exécutées directement moyennant paiement comptant contre connaissement, ou par l'entremise des agences usuelles d'achats.	Le ordinazioni si eseguiscono direttamente a pagamento contanti contro Polizza di Carico, oppure per tramite delle solite vie di compra.	Los pedidos se ejecutan directamente mediante pago al contado contra conocimientos de embarque, o por los medios usuales de compra.	時款肯心布

Unfortunately, the letter written by Kenyons that caused this response from Brierleys was not found on file, but things must have been smoothed over as the two firms continued doing business for some time after this little *contretemps*.

They were not the only firm to be disgruntled. In 1889, Thomas Cresswell & Co of Huddersfield wrote:

> Dear Sirs
> We are much annoyed at not receiving the vestings for our orders 41 and 635 promised for December 1st and unless we receive them by return shall be obliged to cancel. Please report at once ....

These do seem to have been nothing more than the usual 'blips' in business relations, as all the firms continued to be customers for some years.

Jonas Kenyon & Sons

In 1903 a limited company was formed with William Henry Kenyon as the chairman. He was not only a competent businessman. He also patented an 'undermotion for taking the strain off heald shafts when using a negative dobby and this, known as the 'Kenyon' undermotion, was recognised as being a definite improvement on previous systems.'[16] This became widely used in the industry.

Over the years the business outgrew the mill buildings. A plan of 1909 – drawn up for the Fine Art and General Insurance Company Ltd – shows one run of weaving sheds, finishing buildings, a small dyehouse and engine-house. There was a small yard at the front of the mill, but all the rest was open land. A single block of toilets, at the rear of the weaving sheds, served all the mill hands.

By the time a new plan was drawn up for insurance purposes in 1944, there were further weaving sheds, an enlarged engine room and a tall chimney. The mill buildings gradually took up much of the open land. Further space was needed for the engines that provided the power, and further toilet facilities for the expanding workforce. This plan continued to be used as the basis for insurance on the buildings.

Jonas Kenyon & Sons made coatings and vestings, gabardines, worsted and indigo serges. Dyeing of indigo material was quite specialised work and this was often put out to dyers, though some was done by the firm itself. The dye was expensive and had to be conserved wherever possible, so the pieces were wrung out and the dye

Dearnefield Mill in 1909.

MESSRS JONAS KENYON & SONS LTD
DEARNE SIDE MILLS
DENBY DALE
NEAR HUDDERSFIELD

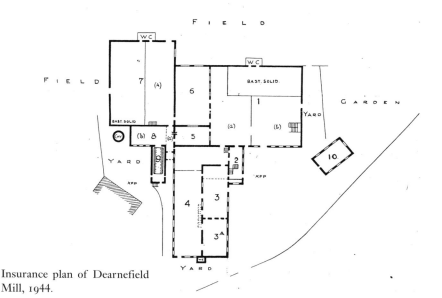

Insurance plan of Dearnefield
Mill, 1944.

recycled, but it was always easy to tell the workers
who worked in the indigo dye sheds – their hands
were dyed almost as blue as the cloth itself.

First World War

When the First World War broke out, many men
volunteered for the Forces, but by 1916 conscription
was brought in. Large employers, such as mill
owners, had to send in a return of all males working
in the mill and the date they started there.[17]

Since most men between 18 and 45 were already
away in the Forces, the remaining males were mostly
young boys awaiting call-up or men of retirement age.
They included George Wood, who was 71 and had
started in the mill in 1899. Others had begun even
earlier – William Heeley, aged 51, had begun there in
1882, whilst Charles Firth, 59, had started in 1885.

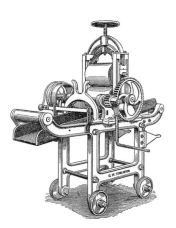

Wringing machine
for indigo cloth.

Some had obviously come back from retirement to work. Robert Clarke and
Benjamin Firth, both aged 68, had started work there only in 1917. At the other end

of the scale, Friend Thorpe, J Heywood and H Horn were only 16, starting work in 1915 before being called up for the war.

The return shows that Jonas Kenyon, the son of William Henry, who had started in the mill at age 17, was the mill manager at the early age of 27, whilst his father, and uncle – Arthy Kenyon – were the managing directors. Jonas' brothers Walter and Wilson were both in the Army.

During this time the firm was making army uniforms in khaki and 'hospital blue'. The blue uniform, just the same rough wool mix as normal uniforms, was worn by soldiers in military hospitals around the country, including the Victoria Memorial Hall, not far away in Denby Dale, which was taken over for the purpose.

The firm did not always have good relations with the local council though. In 1824 the Shepley Lane Head had been turnpiked – a private enterprise method of maintaining the road, by which a toll could be charged to anyone using it. When the local council took over the turnpike in 1888, they also took over a culvert made by the Turnpike Trustees to carry a stream that otherwise ran over open land belonging to Jonas Kenyon.

In 1929 this stream flooded, causing considerable damage to some of Kenyons' goods. The firm sued the council for the damage, which they said included:

Extract from return of men not at war, made by Kenyon & Sons, 1917.

Hospital workers and patients in 'Hospital Blue' cloth.

1654 lbs [750kg] of yarn, which was washable but not all reusable
127 pieces which had to be rescoured and refinished
470 rolling boards spoilt
3920 lbs [1,778kg] of press paper spoilt
and a brick wall which had to be knocked down and rebuilt.

The total cost of this came to £354 4s. 8d. (£354.23). According to the firm, the council had failed to strengthen the culvert when the road was widened and raised.

However, when Jonas Kenyon had purchased the land in 1854, part of the agreement was that he would 'scour, cleanse and keep in repair the said intended water course or drain'.[18] The council counterclaimed that, as Kenyons had culverted part of the stream, it was that part which was responsible for the damage.[19]

Local People

As was often the case in the nineteenth and early twentieth centuries, many workers stayed with the firm from starting work to retiring. Wright Beaumont, born in Scissett in 1871, began at the mill as an apprentice mechanic. He was earning the grand sum of 7s. (35p) by 1887 and the following year this rose to 9s. (45p), continuing to increase by a shilling or two each year. By the time he finished his apprenticeship at age 21, he was earning 16s. a week (80p). Wright was still working at the mill in 1917.

Most families had many members employed in the local mills. Both the sisters of Charles Firth were 'mill girls', being described as 'shawl fringers' in the census, but

Workers at Kenyon & Sons about 1897.

their grandfather was a stonemason. Charles, as shed foreman, earned a good wage –
24s. (£1.20) in 1887, rising to 28s. (£1.40) two years later. After that his pay did not
increase until almost 12 years later, when Charles had a large increase to 33s. (£1.65).

This seems to have been the case with other workers too. James Waldie had begun
work as a boy in the mill, working his way up the scale to become foreman dyer.
Whilst his wages increased each year up to 1889, they then remained at 22s. (£1.10)
until 1901, when they rose to 28s. (£1.40).[20]

The women mill hands did not earn as much as their male counterparts and, as
was normal for the time, they were not eligible for supervisory jobs. Most seem to
have earned about 9s. or 10s. (45–50 p) per week, though one, Kate Ellis, managed
to earn over £1 on some weeks. The workers were paid 'piece' rates, that is, so much
per piece of cloth woven or mended.

Just as the firm had some troubled times with their customers, industrial relations
were sometimes strained. After the First World War, adjustments had to be made to
workers' pay as agreed by the local committees.

In December 1918, an official of the National Society for Dyers and Finishers
wrote to Kenyons, stating:

> I have been requested by your employees engaged in the dyeing and finishing
> departments to make application to you on their behalf to pay the rate of wages
> and observe the conditions as applied to the Huddersfield Manufacturers and
> Federation of Woollen & Worsted Manufacturers.

The dispute continued, with the union beginning to flex its muscles. In December,
they wrote again, asking for a response to their first letter and saying:

> I am given to understand that you have paid other sections of your operatives
> in accordance with the general agreements for the Trade and we respectfully
> submit that the dyers and finishers are entitled to similar consideration.

Even in the spring of the following year, the firm was still not paying the employees
their full dues and the union became a little more blunt in its comments:

> I shall be glad to hear that you are willing to pay the rates or otherwise I shall
> have to notify the Labour Ministry that a dispute is imminent.

The union certainly can't be accused of acting hastily in this instance, as they were
still trying to negotiate six months after the local wage agreements. It remains a
mystery why Kenyons took so long before paying their dyers and finishers the agreed
rate, when they had obviously paid other sections straightaway.

In 1923 William Henry Kenyon died, leaving his brother Arthy to take over. He
was followed in 1934 by William Henry's son Jonas, who was eventually joined by
his wife Isabel, his eldest son William Wood Kenyon, and his nephew Eric Walter
Kenyon. Another of Jonas' sons – James Richard – also worked in the business.

Like all mills, Dearneside had its characters, one of whom was the odd-job man, Norman Beaumont. One of his jobs was to replace belts, when they slipped off the machinery. This could be difficult in the dyehouse, where the steam rose into the roof and hung like a fog, into which Norman regularly had to disappear.

One day, after he had replaced the belt and got the dyepan working again, he mislaid the ladder and had to hang there 'clagged on' to one of the beams until the workers below finally heard his plaintive cries for help above the noise of the dye vats clanking below.[21]

Local Government

The Kenyon family took an active part in local life. William Henry was a local preacher on the Denby Dale Circuit of the Methodist Church[22] and also stood for election to the local board in 1913. Over 20 years later, Jonas Kenyon was also standing for the Denby Dale Urban District Council, expressing his concern for the state of the water supplies and desire to extend the sewage schemes to the outlying areas of Birds Edge and High Flatts.

He had personal reasons for this concern. In 1922 there had been an outbreak of typhoid in Denby Dale and he had been a victim; but, unlike many in poorer circumstances, Jonas had survived. In his election address he was able to state that he came from a family of 'large rate payers and employers' in the area who for 'three generations' had worked for the local people.[23] He gained an MBE in 1974 for his services to local government.

The firm too was involved in local life. Denby Dale is famous for its gigantic pies, made for special celebrations, and the event was usually opened by a local 'celebrity'. In 1928 that person had been William Wood, Jonas Kenyon's father-in-law.

In 1964 it was Jonas' turn to open the event, when floats were decorated by the various organisations in the area and the one from Kenyons won the trophy. Menders rode on the float in the procession, each dressed in costume reflecting the dates when the various pies had been produced.

Jonas Kenyon (1890–1978).

Kenyon Pie Float entry, 1964.

The pie dish was not the original one though. The gigantic dish used in 1887 and 1896 had been auctioned off in 1940, then used for munitions.[24]

Final Days

The beginning of the 1970s seemed positive – cloth woven by the firm was made up into a suit which won the King Edward III Chalice at the National Wool Textile Export Corporation in Paris. The material was described as an '11- or 12-ounce [310–340g] weight of light brown with bright orange overcheck'.[25] At this time over half the firm's production was sold abroad and the trademark of 'Cloth by Kenyon' was known around the world.

But it became impossible to compete with foreign imports and in 1977 production was stopped after continual losses and the mill closed. Eventually the mills were demolished and the site is now covered with housing.

The mill engine was put up for auction and the Northern Mill Engine Society made a desperate bid to save it. It was described as a 150hp vertical cross-compound engine, built in 1900 by an engineering firm in the Huddersfield area and considered an important example of its kind. An appeal was made for funds and an anonymous donor put forward £700, which enabled the society to buy and restore the engine.[26] It is now believed to be in Halifax Museum.

Kirkheaton Mills

Originally just a dyehouse, Kirkheaton Mill was at one time called Shop Lane Mills. It was developed and expanded by the Ainley family, hence its occasional name of Ainley's Mill.

Richard Ainley was a small-time clothier and weaver in the district in the 1780s, when his son Joseph was born. In 1796 the lad 'was apprenticed to learn the mystery of the art of weaving and his indentures entitled him to 14 days instruction at the Grammar School'.[27] This may be where the family gained their lifelong interest in education and support for local schools.

Seven years later, the indentures expired and Joseph began work as a weaver. As a fully skilled worker, Joseph was considered an eligible bachelor so it is not surprising that he soon married. His wife's name was Frances Hefford, hence his first-born son's unusual Christian name.

Ordnance Survey map 1893: scale 25″ to 1 mile.

As the trade expanded and developed, Joseph's skill grew and by 1841 he could describe himself as a 'fancy weaver', producing the intricate patterns popular on waistcoats of the time. He also went on to become a farmer in a small way, as did many clothiers. His son, Hefford, was able to train as a designer of fancy patterns;[28] he was ambitious and wanted his own business. By 1869 he had achieved that aim.

Deeds of 1865 and 1866[29] show that Amos Tyas, manufacturer, in partnership with a cloth finisher called Joseph Smith of Marsh, bought land in Shop Lane, Kirkheaton, from members of the Senior family. It had a house and garden, warehouse, press shop, store and reeling room, cart shed, stable and yard. There was also a dyehouse, with two closes of land.

Amos Tyas was already using the buildings and land, but the sale also included seven cottages on 2 acres (0.8ha) of land. These cottages were occupied by weavers and mill hands, so it is likely that they worked in the dyehouse.

Many small clothiers did not have the space, equipment or capital to dye their own cloth. It required vats of dyestuff, and machines or tubs to immerse the yarn or cloth, and it was a dirty, smelly, messy business. When lengths of cloth were completed, the clothier took his fabric to the local dyehouse, where it was dyed for him and could then be

Weaver's cottage at Kirkheaton Mill.

Kirkheaton Mill.

taken to the cloth hall and sold. The whole piece was dyed in a single colour, but changes were made as technology advanced and fashions changed.

In 1869, the land, dyehouse and cottages were again sold,[30] this time to the partnership of Hefford Ainley and William Henry Lord, both of Huddersfield, fancy cloth manufacturers. The buildings were still not described as a mill at this point. It is likely that the partnership built the mill soon after their purchase of the dyehouse, as a mill is specifically referred to in a further deed of 1878.[31]

The windows in the main part of the mill look reminiscent of a church and this is because the architect was mainly concerned with ecclesiastical buildings. Further land near to the reservoir was bought in 1903,[32] probably to obtain better access for maintenance.

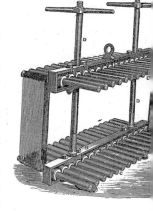

More of the workers now needed to work inside the mill itself. Instead of completing the cloth and then dyeing it, the yarn was dyed first and a pattern woven into the cloth by mixing the different coloured yarns.

The Ainley family were very much involved in the business, knowing all their workers and appearing at the mill on a daily basis. Mrs Ainley also visited the workers' cottages, just as the squire and his wife would have done on country estates. The workers' cottages were all kept scrupulously clean, except the weaving chamber which was always a bit dirty because of the oil needed for weaving.

The 1871 census specifically mentions that Hefford Ainley employed 46 hands 'on the premises' and 'about 50 outweavers', proving that home working still went on, as well as work in the mill.

Yarn-stretching machine.

One family source recounts the tale of meeting an old mill worker coming back from church one day and, on asking how he was and where he'd come from, was told that he'd had some troubles so he'd been to 'talk trouble over w' maister'. He'd been at Hefford Ainley's graveside, at Kirkheaton church.

Kirkheaton church.

Hefford Ainley was a local historian as well as manufacturer and wrote his own history of Kirkburton and Dogley Lane Sunday schools, both of which he was involved in setting up. He was a firm believer in the value of instilling Christian principles in young people to keep them on the straight and narrow, so as to 'conspire to instil into the youthful bosom principles and sentiments that will operate as preventatives to vice, and antidotes to the contagion of vicious examples'.[33]

In 1882 the Earl of Dartmouth, one of the principal landowners in the area, laid the foundation stone of St John's School, Kirkburton, 'on a plot of ground about 2000 square yards in area, the gift of Mr Hefford Ainley who has already formed the streets abutting thereon'. The school had a T-shaped plan, with a large room 36 × 22ft (11 × 6.7m) in the bottom part and two classrooms 20ft (6.1m) square in the top part. There were also a lobby and cloakroom for the scholars' use, with room for 200 infants.

Even at that time, the designers had recognised who would be running the important things in life. The school is described as having a copper boiler for tea meetings but 'The hot water ... is so arranged as to be drawn on the school floor level so as not to necessitate the ladies (who usually manage these things) going down in the cellar'.[34]

In addition to the land, Hefford Ainley gave over £50 worth of stone and the firm donated £215 towards the building costs. The school had oak beams inside, but must have been quite low since a description suggests that a tall person could stretch up and touch the beams of the floor above. There were windows at either end, but one wall was built into the excavated side of the hill, making the room very gloomy. Dark oak benches and desks could not have added to the cheeriness of the place.

Hefford and his sons, John and Joseph, served as churchwardens at Kirkheaton church, making donations to various improvements and extensions. Early in 1872, Hefford made a donation towards the purchase of the turret clock. In 1886 a fire broke out in the church and the company's fire engine had to come promptly to the rescue. The dark old seating used by the Sunday school children was completely destroyed as was most of the west gallery, but all was rebuilt in the following year, with the Ainley family giving generously towards the costs as usual.

When Hefford's wife, Martha, died, he had a window in the church dedicated to her memory. It depicted 'the bringing of young children to Christ that He may bless them'. Hefford Ainley died in October 1909 and is buried in Kirkheaton church alongside his wife.

The two sons had taken over the family firm but finally decided to retire from business and sold the mill premises to Broadhead and Graves Ltd.[35] The new firm had already decided to change the name of the

Broadhead & Graves drawing.

mills which 'heretofore [were] known as Shop Lane Mills but intended to be known as Kirkheaton Mills formerly in the occupation of Ainley Sons & Co Ltd.'

The Broadhead family had worked in the textile industry for many years, starting in Holmfirth but later moving down to Lockwood. George Henry Broadhead was an overlooker there, in charge of a small group of workers, but eventually became a manager. His efforts gave him the finance needed to ensure that his eldest son, Fred, was able to become a designer.

Fred proved to be a hard worker and was prepared to put in the many hours needed to build up the business, producing a variety of designs for the cloth. He was, apparently, just as hard on his son, Frank, who not only worked at the mill but also spent his evenings doing paperwork for his father. Nor was the lad spared the indignity of being jabbed with a sharp pin if he fell asleep over his books.[36]

In 1919 Fred Broadhead died, leaving Frank to take over the business at the young age of 28, together with Mr Graves and a new director, E M Johnson, a pattern designer.

The firm expanded rapidly and added further buildings. These were the source of much pride when the Duke of York visited the mill in 1932. He was shown around every department – from sorting the wool, through cleaning, spinning, weaving and tentering to dry and check the cloth, right up to final mending and packing.

In 1964,[37] a fire broke out in the mill and all the patterns and design records from the earliest days of firm were lost. Over 50 firemen were needed to tackle the blaze and 'Flames from the burning mill which is situated on the top of a hill made a beacon which could be seen as far away as Dewsbury and Linthwaite'. Although the alarm had been raised quickly, within half an hour the roof of the three-storey building collapsed.

As this happened, all the machinery plunged down to the bottom of the building. The road had to be closed for a while and the spectacle brought people from miles around. Once it was obvious that nothing could be done to save the pattern

A tentering machine with operative.

department, the firemen concentrated on stopping the fire spreading, especially to the new office block.

The fire caused local controversy, when questions were raised about the lack of water. Only the fact that water was available from the mill dam saved the rest of the buildings and the local council had to set about improving the water supply to the area.

Although most workers could continue, some weavers had to be sent home until alternative arrangements could be made. One worker, Irven Lodge, who had been with the firm for 32 years, having worked there from leaving school, commented that one new loom, lost in the fire, hadn't even been used, as the mill was one of the most up-to-date in Huddersfield, having a big export trade with America.

The arrangements made for the workers were typical of the 'interweaving' of the textile trade in Huddersfield. Space and machines were rented at Wellington Mills in Oakes – the place vacated previously by Martin & Sons, who were to join Broadhead & Graves in Kirkheaton Mills at a later date.

The following year, a new weaving shed and design department were built and the firm were soon producing up-to-the-minute designs again, influenced now by new pop groups such as the Beatles and by Carnaby Street fashions.

Top fashion designers came from America 'because British wool cloths were the best in the world' and they came looking for brighter colours and bolder designs.[38] Fashion designers from Europe and Japan also visited the firm over the years. The firm continued in business during the lean years of the 1970s and 1980s, concentrating on its niche market of high-quality worsteds and exporting most of its production.

The site is now owned by Illingworth Morris (Saltaire) and is home to the trade names of Learoyds, Martin & Sons, Josiah France, Yates and Huddersfield Fine Worsteds, who still produce high-quality worsteds for Savile Row and for export.

Broadhead & Graves
cloth badge.

Modern machinery in Kirkheaton mill.

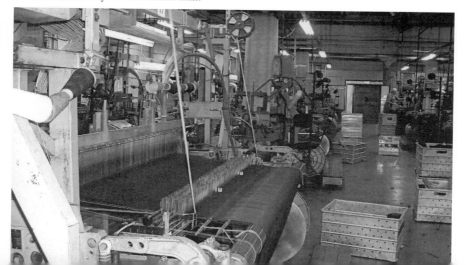

Linfit Mill

Linfit Mill was built about the beginning of the nineteenth century. It is quite unusual in that it was built specifically to take advantage of the coalfields to the south-east of Huddersfield. It is in an area where there is very little water power, with no major rivers or large brooks.

In 1734 a lease[39] was drawn up between Lady Ann Kaye, relict of Sir Arthur Kaye of Woodsome in Almondbury, and Abraham Hey, the elder of Thorncliffe in Kirkburton, clothier, for a messuage and tenements called Capon Croft, Far Knowle, Middle Knowle, Birks Impley and Wheat Ing. The rent was £8 4s. 4d. (£8.22), with another £3 for a mill in Burton for grinding corn, grain and malt. Abraham also agreed that he would 'carry all cloth which shall be made upon the premises to the fulling mills in Honley in the said parish of Almondbury'.

George Hey & Sons

Abraham Hey, who leased the mill from Lady Kaye in 1734, was probably an ancestor of the George Hey who eventually took over Linfit Mills.

The mills had been let to the partnership of Smith and Hampshire but, in 1817, David Smith and Joseph Hampshire filed for bankruptcy and a notice appeared in the *Leeds Mercury* to order them to appear before the Commission of Bankruptcy in Wakefield, and then in Liversedge in the afternoon to declare all their assets, and for their creditors to appear to prove their debts.

As a result of this, an auction was held in May of the machinery in Linfit Mill. The machinery was described as 'all nearly new, of the latest Construction, in most excellent Condition and well clothed with Cards for the working of fine wools.'

The Assignees of the bankrupt were also looking for someone to take over the lease of the mill itself, possibly together with the purchase of the machinery which was 'worked by an Engine of 21 horse power, near to excellent Coal, in the Centre of a Manufacturing District, only Four Miles from the trading Town of Huddersfield, and where Hands are plentiful and Labour moderately cheap'.

Linfit Mill.

By this date, George Hey was already in business and making money. In 1815 he was dealing in land and bought some land in Thorncliffe Green, Kirkburton, which had been allotted to Thomas Allen of Gledholt under the Enclosure Act.[40] Although the initial cost was only £10, it was agreed that a further fee of £470 would be paid.

It is possible that this new-found wealth came from the recent death of his father, who in 1810 had named his sons – Abraham, George, John and Robert – as residuary legatees of his goods. It may have been at this time that George Hey moved into Linfit Mill but certainly in 1836 he was receiving rent for the premises[41] from Benjamin Cocker, Joah Sugden and James Womersley, who presumably were renting parts of the mill (referred to as Linthwaite Mill).

During this time the mills were insured with the Globe Insurance Company and there are records of costs of repairs and general maintenance undertaken by Benjamin Cocker and Joah Sugden.

The Factory Commission Inquiry

The Factory Commission inquiry of 1834 produced a report – published as Parliamentary Papers (House of Commons) 1834, *Employment of Children in Factories* – that is full of incidental detail about the mills of the Yorkshire woollen district.

The commission interviewed Benjamin Cocker, who described the work in Linfit Mill as 'Wool scribbled, carded and slubbed and woollen pieces milled'. According to him, the old mill had been erected about 1800, the new mill about 1813. Steam power was used, with an engine of 20hp. It also powered two grindstones, which were leased off.

They had twenty-two employees, fifteen men and boys with seven girls. There is a marked contrast in wages. The two boys and two girls under 10 all received the same wage of 6s. (30p) each; but the girls between 10 and 14 received only 3s. each (15p), whereas the boys aged 10 to 12 continued to be paid 6s. (30p) and the older boys were paid 12s. (60p). Surprisingly, the oldest boys aged over 14 received only 7s. (35p), yet the girls of the same age group earned 10s. (50p). There were no women over 21, but all the men earned £3 14s. 6d. (£3.72½).

There was no breakfast time allowed, despite starting work at 6.30 am but other breaks included half an hour for drinking at 10 am, one hour for dinner at 12.30 and half an hour for drinking at 4.30. The firm seemed to have a relaxed attitude to rules – sometimes sickness was paid for, sometimes not; sometimes the workers had to make up lost time after an accident, not at others. Presumably it depended on the whim of the manager at the time.

Holidays included Christmas, when three days were given; 'Fastness' which was given half a day; Easter had two half-days; and at Trinity there were three days. Again, some workers had these holidays paid, some did not; but there was no explanation as to who was paid, or why.

When asked about the treatment of children, Cocker replied that corporal punishment was sanctioned but not beyond reason 'nor can it be dispensed with at all times'. He felt that 'The nature of our work requires children to be employed under 12 years of age; their employment is in piecing cardings.'

Kirkburton church and Hey grave.

George Hey Senior and Junior

By 1847 the rents of £135 were split between George Hey, who received half the amount, and Edward Ellis and William Carter who shared the other half.

In 1855 George Hey and William Carter leased[42] coal and mineral rights near Linthwaite Lane. These mines must have been used for a long time as the lease lists previous leaseholders back to 1810. Having their own supply of coal was an obvious advantage to the mill. It cut their costs and reduced their dependence on others.

The rents distribution was changed again in 1858, when they were split evenly between George Hey and William Carter. But in this year George Hey sr died and was buried in Kirkburton churchyard. The business was taken over by his son George jr, and his grandsons John Tucker, Charles and George.

George senior's will[43] left small sums of money to his daughters Harriet Nowell, a widow, and Ann Ramsden, wife of Thomas Ramsden of Ramsden Mill in Linthwaite, with all the household furniture and effects to be divided between his son George and the two daughters. Presumably, George junior also received the pew in Kirkburton Church, which his father had bought in 1835 for £13.

Like many other wealthy men, George Hey took part in local parish council business and in 1868 was at the centre of a local row, when he was accused of not being

George Hey, taken about 1880.

Public Apology published 1868.

entirely honest in his dealings. He seems to have won his case, though, because on 1 May an apology was published.

Disaster

Mills are, of course, dangerous places and particularly vulnerable to fire. There was no Fire Brigade to call; everyone relied on friends and neighbours to help or, in the case of a business, the insurance company employed its own fire engine, which their customers could send for.

PUBLIC APOLOGY.

I, JOHN BINNS, of Riley, Kirkburton, Farmer, hereby confess that I was not justified in making the statements I have made against Mr. GEORGE HEY and Mr. JOHN PARKIN, as to their having misappropriated monies belonging to The Local Board of Kirkburton, and I HUMBLY APOLOGISE to, for having uttered such statements; and I agree to pay all expenses.

As witness my hand this 1st day of May, 1868.

(Signed) JOHN BINNS.

Witness,
GEORGE DYSON,
    Solicitor, Huddersfield.

GEO. HARPER, CHRONICLE STEAM PRINTING WORKS, HUDDERSFIELD.

In 1864 the *Huddersfield Chronicle* carried the story of the destruction of part of the mill:[44]

> At an early hour on Monday morning last, a fire occurred at this mill [Linfit Mill], the property of Messrs George Hey and Wm Carter, woollen manufacturers, which for a time threatened to prove of serous consequences. In the mill yard running at right angles with the large and extensive mills is a small detached building, only fifteen feet from the main building, used as a store room for waste, etc. It is two storeys high and 10 windows long, the gable end running close up to the road side.
>
> About a quarter past three o'clock, James Smith, the private watchman on the premises, discovered flames issuing through the lower windows of that portion of the building nearest the public road and in which was a large quantity of waste, dye stores etc as well as waste cleaning machine or 'willow'. He immediately gave the alarm, when Mr Hey was soon on the spot.
>
> Seeing the danger, he immediately despatched his son on horseback to Huddersfield for the Leeds and Yorkshire engine, which reached the place about half-past five. They were soon in play, the object being to preserve the adjoining buildings. In this they were successful, but not before one half of the low detached building with its contents were destroyed. In the upper storey were placed a number of carding machines and 'billeys' which were out of use. These, together with the buildings were destroyed. The damage is estimated at about £200 which is partially covered by insurance in the Leeds and Yorkshire office.

In December 1867 James Smith, a banksman at the coal pit, had an accident. The pit was only a short distance from the mill, but to save time a tramway had been laid from the pit right up to the engine-house of the mill. When the coal 'corves' (wagons) were loaded, the weight of the coal would enable the trucks to roll down the hill at speed.

Smith rode on the truck in order to apply the brakes and prevent the trucks running into anything. Unfortunately, he overbalanced and fell off the truck, hitting his face on the rails. No bones were broken and he was treated for cuts and bruises. The report doesn't say what happened to the truck!

The machinery in the mill was the cause of often gruesome accidents. One employee, Joseph Mosley, was attending to one of the machines, when his clothes were caught by it and his right arm was drawn in and torn from his shoulder. Charles Hey immediately went for a surgeon, who had to complete the amputation of the arm at the scene of the accident before the poor man could be taken to the Huddersfield Royal Infirmary.[45]

Heyday and Last Days

In 1877 George Hey & Sons leased[46] from William Lodge a mine, coal seam and land in the area, to enhance the supply of coal for their engine. This continued until 1891 when the three grandsons re-leased the mine to James Hall.

In 1879 the insurance with Mutual Fire Insurance Corporation shows the mill to have been valued at £6,630 with a premium of £56 12s. 11d. (£56.65). The insurance covered:

fireproof first floor, two storeys in height; occupied for cloth cutting, brushing, burling, a cloth warehouse and offices

machinery

stock

building of non fireproof second floors, handloom pattern weaving and warping

boiler house and cloth drying store and other buildings

Dyeplants and tentering machines

The building of stone or brick built and slated or tiled known as Linfit Mills, Kirkburton

Heated and worked by steam

Not working between 9 pm and 5 am

Mixtures of wool, cotton but no shoddy or mungo

KC313/6/3

Whether the mill was fireproof or not had a considerable effect on the insurance premium, and most new mills were built with brick roofs between the floors, and cast iron girders in support rather than the wood structures of earlier mills.

The year 1888 saw the need for premises in Huddersfield, leading to an agreement between John Tucker and Charles to rent a room in Bulstrode Buildings from Sir John William Ramsden at a rate of £25 per year. Initially in No 21, they moved in 1891 to No 5 in the same buildings. These offices were essential to give a central point of contact for their customers and to provide a base for the managers to use in town. Most mills in the area also had offices or warehouses in the centre of Huddersfield.

Not everything went smoothly in the family, however. In 1896 John Tucker signed an agreement not to mortgage property unlawfully, being paid off with a one-off sum of £150 and a stern warning not to ask for a further advance. Presumably he had been raising money without the agreement of the others in the family business.

The remaining members of the family eventually decided not to continue in the business and in 1897 there was a lease[47] of Linfit Mill agreed between John Tucker Hey, William Stringer, book-keeper, James Tideswell of Frizinghall, gent, woolstapler (trustees under the will of George Hey deceased) and the Pentonville Stamping and Engineering Co, London.

In 1900, an advertisement appeared in the *Huddersfield Examiner* for the sale or lease of Linfit Mill, which included the mill buildings, land, boiler and engine, together with a number of 'lots' of land and other premises in the area, which the family and business had acquired over the years. Wright Blackburn & Co, hearth rug manufacturer, was operating from the mill at the beginning of the twentieth century.[48]

The last of the coal was worked in 1927 and the mill finally closed soon after. Linfit became one of the earliest mills in the area to find a new use. An application was made to convert the mill into 19 residential units with garages, and this was agreed. The buildings have been preserved and cleaned, and their future is secured. The whole area has now been landscaped.

Other Mills in the Area

Almondbury township

Birks Mill	An early fulling and scribbling mill on the Dartmouth estates, used by Messrs Nowell, Cockhill & Bennett in 1837 as well as John Nowell & Sons.[49]
Hole Bottom Mills	At the bottom of Almondbury Bank, this small mill housed Dundas Rug & Textiles Ltd in the middle of the twentieth century.
King's Mill	Manorial fulling mill used in 1857 by Joseph Varley. By the twentieth century, it housed a variety of textile firms. The area now has many new industrial units built over it.
Northfield Mill	Used in the 1860s by J E Taylor & Bros. Sykes & Tunnacliffe, mohair yarn spinners, operated from this mill up to the mid-twentieth century. Area is now given over to housing.
Queen's Mill	John Marsden leased this mill *c.*1860 and raised it from three to six storeys. By 1910 Brook & Woodhouse Ltd were here and remained until the mid-twentieth century.
St Helen's Mill	This was a dyeworks in 1860 but little is known about its history. It was for sale in 1867 when it was described as being in the occupation of Messrs Spivey & Sons.[50]
Taylor Hill Mill	An early mill, where Frank Vickerman was attacked by Luddites in 1812. The Yorkshire Textiles Directory [hereafter

Taylor Hill Mill.

YTD] shows B Vickerman & Sons still here in 1910, along with Bruck & Englemann. Mill now divided into units, which have some textile use.

Clayton West township
Spring Grove Mill   Built at the beginning of Victoria's reign by William Norton and later taken over by the Beanland family.

Cumberworth township
Blue Slate Mills   Also known as Greenhouse Mill, this was put up for sale in 1867 when it was in the occupation of Thomas Armitage;[51] little else is known about this mill.

Elm Mill   The Field family were responsible for many of the mills in Skelmanthorpe. This one housed the business of Frank W Field. Now partly converted to flats.

Garrett Mills   Built by the Field family and used by W & J Field.

Elm Mill.

Greenhouse Mills	See Blue Slate Mill.
Greenside Mill	Built *c.*1770 by William Marsden. His daughter married Richard Field, who traded there for a number of years until forming the partnership of Field & Bottrill in the 1880s. Now Dawson Fabrics Ltd.
Nortonthorpe Mills	Norton family. Still in use by the same firm.
Tenter Croft Mills	See Garrett Mills.

Dalton township

Bradley Mills	An early fulling mill, FCR 1834 showed it in use for slubbing, carding, weaving etc. The Atkinson family used this mill from about the 1840s onwards; other firms also rented parts. Messrs Carter & Cocker were here in 1878.[52] In the twentieth century, it has housed Sellers, Lister & Co; Ralph Wood & Co.
Dalton Mills	Brierley & Wall, yarn spinners, occupied this mill *c.*1881. They seem to have moved to Cowmes Mill, Lepton, by the 1890s. Mapplestone & Wilkinson Ltd were here in 1910.
Green Lea Mills	Westfield Cotton Ltd were in this mill in 1950. It is now industrial units.
Greenside Mills	At the end of the nineteenth century, this mill was home to George Wilson & Co, silk spinners, later being taken over by Dyson, Hall & Co, who made pile fabrics. It recently burned down; houses are now built on the site.
Mill Hill Mill	Occupied by the Tolson Brothers in the 1870s.
Rookery Mills	Built *c.*1840 when J Dransfield & Sons were here; the firm of Tolson, Haigh & Brook leased part of the mill *c.*1870. It was home to Fred Chrispin & Co up to the mid-1970s.
Storth's Mill	John Day was in this mill in 1848 (see Bankfield Mill, Moldgreen) but it was owned by the Tolson family. It was leased to Josiah Naylor, hearth rug manfacturer, in 1910. Lawton & Lodge Ltd were here in 1950.
Westfield Mill	Jonathan Beaumont & Son are listed as shoddy & mungo merchants in this mill in 1910.

Denby Dale township

Birds Edge Mill	Hirst Brothers were here in the mid-1800s, Child & Co by 1890 and F H McGrath in 1910.
Cuttlehurst Mill	A later mill, built about the end of the nineteenth century, when L T Crowther & Co were here; J Blackburn & Sons here in 1910.
Hartcliffe Mill	Z Hinchliffe & Co, woollen and worsted manufacturers, began in this mill and it is still used by them.
Inkerman Mill	James Peace was an early occupier. John Brownhill & Co Ltd, woollen and worsted manufacturers, were in the mill by 1910 and also in Springfield Mills, Kirkburton.

Lower Putting Mill/ Pudding Mill	See Pudding Mill.
Pudding Mill	An old fulling mill, this is an early example of a mill put to other uses. It was converted to cottages about the middle of the nineteenth century.
Springfield Mill	Now units and mill shops.

Farnley Tyas township

Farnley Mill	A fulling and scribbling mill on the Dartmouth estates, it was built by Roberts & Co, who were also the tenants. It is an early example of a mill installing a steam engine (in 1805) because of poor water supply. FCR 1834 shows the mill occupied by Roberts, Kay & Dyson, but in the 1850s it was taken over by Herman Geissler & Sons from Germany. The firm went bankrupt in the late 1880s.

Kirkburton township

Beehive Mill	Joab Ramsden Brook was one of the early occupiers of this mill; Daniel Brook was in the mill from the 1870s for about twenty years. It was then sold and no longer used for the textile trade.
Brookfield Mill	This was originally a rope & twine manufacturer called Dan Brook, but 1910 YTD shows Singleton & Co Ltd, woollen manufacturers, were here. Pape & Sons Ltd moved here from Paddock c.1950.
Burton Mills	See Dogley Lane Mill.
Carter Mill	In 1910, Gustav Geissler Ltd was here (see Farnley Mills). By 1950 Whitworth's Textiles had taken over the mill.
Dogley Lane Mill	An early fulling and scribbling mill on the Dartmouth estates, used by Jonas & James Kenyon for many years. YTD 1910 shows Liversedge & Co and Allen R Dyson, merino spinners. Thompson Woollen Manufacturing Co Ltd had replaced them by the mid-twentieth century.
Green Grove Mill	Built c.1833, this was first just a two-storey handloom weaving shed, not mechanised until its expansion about the end of the nineteenth century. Sydney H Shaw & Co Ltd were here in 1950; now a clothing manufacturers.
Linfit Mills	See main text above.
Moxon's Mill	See Southfield Mills.
Southfield Mills	B H Moxon Ltd used this mill for some time. Proposed to build houses on this site, subject to planning permission.
Springfield Mill	Wright Rhodes from Saddleworth bought this mill in 1845. By 1876 it had been sold to Hirst Hanson & Sons. B H Moxon & Sons took the mill c.1910 and remained until recently. Now industrial units.

Kirkheaton Mills	See main text above.
Levi Mill	At the end of the eighteenth century, Levi Stead leased land to build a mill. The 1848 Trade Directory shows Abraham Sheard in the mill.

Lepton township

Cowmes Mill	Also known as Spa Mill and built *c.*1830, it housed various firms including Abraham Brierley, who went into partnership to form Rhodes & Brierley of Vale Mills. The firm of Rowland Mitchell & Co were in the mill for the first half of the twentieth century.
Fenay Mill	A fulling mill on the Dartmouth estate leased to Dan Brook, who was followed by a younger relative, George Brook. The firm of Bentley & Sykes was here at the start of the twentieth century but it is now a restaurant.
Rowley Mill	This was a fulling and scribbling mill on the Dartmouth estates in the 1790s. The firm of J & T Kenyon were in the mill for many years at the end of the nineteenth century, when it was sold to George Beaumont & Sons.
Spa Mill	See Cowmes Mill.
Vale Mill	Also known as Tandem Sheds. Built in 1880s by the firm of Rhodes & Brierley.
Whitley Willows Mill	Mill built *c.*1780. Tolson Bros moved here in the 1850s. Glendinning Brothers also spent some time here before moving to the town centre (see Tanfield Mills). Though the mill buildings are no longer used for textile production, it is hoped to find a use for them.

Moldgreen township

Bankfield Mills	See main text above.
Birkhouse Mill	Godfrey Sykes & Sons were making sealskins and plush fabrics for soft toys and teddy bears here in the early twentieth century. Wm Siswick, waste pullers, were in this mill in 1910.

Scissett township

Ings Mill	Established in 1890, the firm of Edward Blackburn Ltd used this mill.

Shelley township

Barncliffe Mills	In 1950 this mill housed Shelley Textiles Ltd, Tweed & Co Ltd and England & Co (Shelley) Ltd.
Brookhouse Mill	William Child & Co, rug manufacturers, were here *c.*1900.
Woodhouse Mill	Ben North was in this scribbling mill in the 1790s. FCR 1834 shows the firm of Ben Fitton & Sons, who were still there in

the 1870s when Messrs Tolson, Haigh & Brook leased part of the mill.

Shepley township

Firth Mill	Demolished *c.*1978.
Shepley New Mill	Another mill associated with the Kenyon name – James Kenyon was here in 1859. The firm became Barnicot & Kenyon, but by 1910 Firth Bros were at the mill.
Victoria Mill	Often called a warehouse, this was an early dyehouse but in use as a textile mill by Ben Armitage & Sons by the 1880s. W & E Armitage are listed in 1910 and are still here in 1950 alongside Ben Armitage & Sons.
Whitby Mills	Listed in 1910 for Benjamin Armitage & Sons Ltd, woollen & worsted manufacturers.

Chapter Five
Holme Valley

South of Huddersfield, the deep valleys of the River Holme and its tributaries contained many mills, from Lockwood and Newsome on the edge of the town to Holmbridge, above Holmfirth, and beyond. Reservoirs were built to give the force needed and ensure a year-round supply of water power. The river was not easily tamed and the Holmfirth Flood in 1852 took many lives and much property was destroyed, including a number of mills. Up the sides of the valleys are rows of housing, many with the multiple-windowed top storey of the weavers' cottages.

Typical weavers' cottages of Hinchliffe Mill.

Albert Mills

In common with Slaithwaite and other places, Lockwood's claim to fame in the early nineteenth century was as a spa. The Bath Hotel was built, together with spa buildings, and White's Trade Directory of 1837 described the area as:

> Lockwood, now celebrated for its Spa is a large, well built and pleasant village, delightfully seated in the valley of the Holme, near its confluence with the other branch of the river Colne, 1 mile south of Huddersfield. Its elegant and commodious Spa Baths built in 1827 in a finely sequestered spot, within half a mile of Huddersfield.
>
> The water is highly esteemed for its medicinal virtues in glandular, rheumatic gouty dyspeptics corbutic and other cutaneous complaints.

Unfortunately, manufacturers were also quick to spot a good opportunity. The water could provide power and clean the wool, and waste could be emptied into the fast-flowing river. Mills began to appear in the area, and Lockwood's hopes of being a beautiful spa resort were quickly dashed.

Albert Mills were built about 1853, as is seen from the ornate dating stone at the entrance. This entrance was actually built considerably later, but it included this original date. Little is known about the original building but it may have been the mill occupied by David Marsden, which was burned down in the early 1850s and rebuilt.[1] In 1856 it was leased to Josiah Berry and Joseph Brooke Turner.

Albert Mill entrance way with datestone above.

Berry & Turner

Josiah Berry came from a long-established family in the area. He was a younger son of Godfrey and Sarah Berry, baptised in 22 April 1826 in Lockwood church, where his elder brother, Godfrey, had also been baptised seven years earlier.

Josiah's father, Godfrey senior, had purchased land in Lockwood during the 1840s, including land on which a 'Chapel or Meeting House' had been erected. This seems to have been bought as 'lots' and later further shares in the land were sold, possibly as a means of raising money. Earlier deeds had referred to 'land belonging to John Berry', so the family seem to have been fairly well off.

Earlier members of the family had owned mills in Honley and were involved in local politics. Godfrey Berry senior went into partnership with Henry Crowther, purchasing Broadfield Mills in Lockwood in 1845,[2] and it seems that Josiah also had some interest in this business.

After his father's death, Josiah – with Alfred and Henry Crowther – purchased the land and mill of Broadfield Mills in Lockwood with the agreement of Samuel Naylor, who was the executor of the late Godfrey Berry's will.[3] Josiah was described in 1851 as 'employer of 208'. At this time he lived in Yews Hill, just above the mills at Lockwood, with his wife, Jane, and children, Charles Albert and Sarah.

Josiah's interest in Broadfield Mill must have been sold later, when the firm of Henry Crowther & Sons began. Kaye and Stewart later took over Broadfield Mills and became one of the largest employers in Huddersfield. Josiah Berry went into partnership with J B Turner.

Like so many other manufacturers, Josiah took his civil duties seriously, serving on the local board at Lockwood. He was a member of the Baptist Church and the Liberal Club of Lockwood.

Much of Lockwood was owned by a syndicate, headed by Robert Bentley, who was also involved with the local brewery. The syndicate bought, sold and leased land in the area, including the Albert Mills. A deed of 6 October 1856 leases land to 'Josiah Berry of Lockwood, woollen cloth manufacturer and Joseph Brooke Turner of Huddersfield, woollen cloth manufacturer' and describes the layout of the land with New Street to the north, land occupied by John William and Henry Shaw to the east and the River Holme to the south.

The buildings consisted of 'mill and dyehouse, warerooms, sizing room, stable, sheds and other outbuildings'. What is now referred to as the 'old mill' originally fronted onto New Street (now Albert Street), It was six storeys high and 15 bays long, built in brick, with cast-iron columns, cross-beams and roof to reduce the fire hazard.

The engine-house at the east end of the mill contained a single beam engine giving, in 1867, up to 200hp. The doorway suggests that engines were considered the controlling deities of mills at this time, and so housed in a more ornate building than the rest of the machinery. Power was sent, via a vertical shaft, to every floor of the mill.

Ornate doorway to the machine room, Albert Mill.

The business included most stages of the textile process, but as there were no weaving sheds at this time it is likely that weaving was still done as 'cottage industry' by workers round about.

The dyehouse was replaced in 1871 and a new mill, 11 bays long and 5 wide, was built. The new mill also contained privies for the workers – one on each floor. Whether this was out of consideration for the workers or to ensure that they didn't have to leave the machinery for long is open to question. Certainly there seems to have been little consideration for the environment: it seems the privies emptied directly into the River Holme behind the mill.

At the same time as the new mill, a number of weaving sheds were also built, filling in the land between the back of the old mill and the river. The sheds, 13 bays long and 3 bays wide, show the standard, saw-tooth glazed roofing, which gave maximum light for the weavers, and the rather ornate, cast-iron framework.

The offices that now face Albert Street were also built at this time, together with the elaborate archway carrying the original building date. They allowed more space for the growing amount of paperwork, as well as controlling access to the site.

However, by 1875 the partnership was dissolved and Josiah Berry retired to Harrogate, where he died in 1901.[4] The business continued as Joseph B Turner & Co and secured a loan for a mortgage from the West Riding Union Bank, but in 1882 Turner went into liquidation and the mills were taken over by the bank.

To recoup some of their money, in May 1882 the bank leased part of the mill to Ben Lawton, a yarn manufacturer who lived in Almondbury. He took over the area known as 'the 4th room in the new and old position of Albert Mills and steam power for turning 6 scribblers, 6 condenser carders, 2 pairs of hand Mules, 2 pairs of self acting Mules and on the Ground Floor of the New Mill room and power for one Willey and so much of the ground floor of the Warehouse connected with the said

Iron roof struts, Albert Mill.

Frontage of Albert Mill.

mill for the storing of raw material'. Though the lease was for five years, at a rent of £540 per year, by June the bank had sold the mill to Messrs Brierley Brothers of Ashbrow Mills for £14,000.

Brierley Brothers

The Brierley family were widespread throughout the Huddersfield area. They came originally from Saddleworth, and established branches in the Kirkburton area (Rhodes & Brierley), in the centre of Huddersfield (John L Brierley) and in Lockwood (as Brierley Brothers). Three of the family – Wright, James and Jesse – went into partnership as Brierley Brothers, at first leasing Ashbrow Mills at Fartown.

In 1880 Jesse Wood, the 19-year-old son of Henry Wood of Lepton, met with an accident that caused his immediate death.[5] He was learning to be a scribbling engineer at Ashbrow Mills and was taking a strap off the main shaft when the strap caught his leg and took him round the shaft. One leg was torn off and most of his bones were broken. He was instantly killed.

The inquest recorded a verdict of accidental death, but Mr Brierley promised to adopt means for preventing similar accidents in future. The specific means were not specified, nor did the courts impose any kind of fine. As far as is known, no compensation was offered either.

In 1882 the firm moved to Albert Mills, where their main business was in the spinning

Yarn-scouring machine.

of yarn. Once wool has been sorted, cleaned and then carded, or combed and carded, it can be spun into yarn.

Sometimes the yarn was sold in its natural state for later piece dyeing; sometimes it would be dyed before sale. Brierley produced yarn for other companies on a commission basis, that is, they produced yarn to order, rather than making their own yarn and then finding a buyer.

Brierley Brothers in turn leased out part of the mills – to Allen Mallinson, who was also a yarn spinner, living in Lockwood Road. He took a room on the second floor, a room on the third floor of both the New and Old mills, space for a willeying machine on the ground floor of the New Mill, offices, storing sheds and stabling, all at £580 per year with his landlords supplying steam power and machinery for '3 pairs self-acting mules, 1 pair hand Mules, 7 scribblers and 7 Condensing Carders'.

The landlords also undertook to supply heating for 56 hours per week, which suggests that the mill hands were working long hours. The fire insurance for that year also shows J Stringer leasing the sixth floor of the Old Mill, for woollen carding, with Brierley Bros occupying the fifth floors in both the Old and New mills for mule spinning and the sixth floor of the New Mill for scribbling and carding.

Continued expansion of trade enabled Brierley Brothers to take over the whole of the mill and, when Lawton's lease ran out in 1886, all their tenants appear to have left, at least until 1891 when Messrs Hollingworth & Wood seem to have begun trading from Albert Mills.

Trading as a partnership has its hazards. If the business goes into liquidation, all the personal assets of the partners become liable to be used against the debts of the firm. Not surprisingly, the brothers eventually decided in 1896 to sell the mill to the newly formed company of Brierley Bros Ltd for £13,386.

Further expansion can be seen from an insurance plan dated about 1900. New sheds, the ornate engine room, boiler rooms and new mill buildings can be seen on the plan, together with the offices and warehouses. In the early days of the textile mills, paperwork was at a minimum and bargains were struck on the word of a gentleman.

Over the years, new skills of management, record-keeping and accounting were developed and applied to the more efficient running of the business, and these required specialised rooms to work in. New, noisy equipment – typewriters and telephones – had to be accommodated and visitors had to be received in plush, clean surroundings.

The twentieth century was a time of expansion for many mills, particularly during the First World War, when uniforms were needed. In 1914, more buildings were added on land purchased to the east of the existing mills. The Yorkshire Textile Directory shows Brierley Brothers operating 8,000 spindles from 1910 onwards. By 1986 they were listed as 'spinners of woollen and speciality fibre yarns for weaving and hosiery.'

Twentieth Century

The early 1990s were considered to be a terrible time for the textile business, but by 1992 the firm had begun to expand again and won the International Wool Secretariat's Wool Forum[6] for achieving a 76% increase in productivity. The directors considered the firm's policy of quality and quick response was the right one for the times. It often allowed them to gain orders for small quantities of yarn, which some manufacturers wanted and could not get abroad. Further plans at the time included giving the mills a face-lift, by cleaning the stone and putting in new windows.

The following year, a fire at the mill[7] could have provided a different ending for Albert Mills. Fortunately, modern fire-prevention methods brought the fire under control quickly and, though production stopped for a week because of the electrical switchgear and cables that were damaged in blaze, the mill was soon back in working order. The business is now part of the Brook Group, but still operates from Albert Mills.

Hollingworth & Wood

This firm began leasing part of Albert Mills in 1896 and remained on the site for many years, being shown in the Yorkshire Textile Directory as running over 70 looms, until the 1960s. Then they needed to reduce the number to only 59 looms. They produced fancy weaves, serges and vicuna fabrics. The firm still exists, but in name only, as part of the Brook Group.

HOLLINGWORTH WOOD & CO. LTD.

FANCY WORSTED & WOOLLEN MANUFACTURERS
Albert Mills, HUDDERSFIELD, ENGLAND

Telephone:
491
HUDDERSFIELD

Telegrams and
Cables:
"WOODBINE,
HUDDERSFIELD"

Code:
5th Edition,
A B C

Town Office:
MARKET
STREET
(opposite the
Exchange)

Specialities:
FANCY WORSTED SUITINGS & MIXTURE OVERCOATINGS of all Weights
SERGES and VICUNAS

Orders executed direct by Cash Payment against Bill of Lading, or through the usual buying channels.
Samples sent to responsible Buyers with reference.   Please send copy of order when buying through Merchants.

FABRICANTS DE TISSUS DE LAINE PEIGNÉE ET DE LAINAGES FANTAISIE.	FABRICANTES DE TEJIDOS DE FANTASIA DE ESTAMBRE Y LANA.
Spécialités :	Especialidades :
Tissus de Laine Peignée pour Complets & Tissus Mélangés de Tous Poids pour Pardessus. Serges and Vigognes.	Telas Fantasía de Estambre para Trajes y Paños mezclilla para Gabanes de cualquier peso. Sargas y Vicuñas.
MANIFATTURA DI FILATI E LANA FANTASIA.	
Specialità :	
Filati Fantasia Stoffe per abiti e misti per Cappotti di tutti pesi. Serge & Vigogna.	

Letterhead of Hollingworth Wood & Co.

Ordnance Survey map 1907: scale 25" to 1 mile.

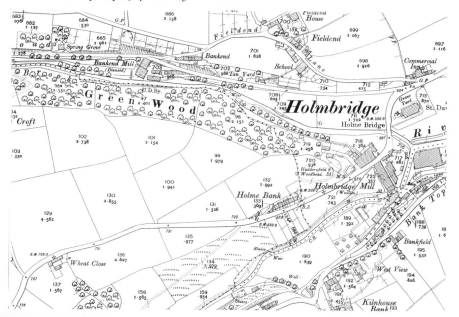

Holmbridge Mill
The Fulling Mill

Holmbridge Mill was built in the 1790s as a water-powered fulling and scribbling mill.[8] As was often the case with these early mills, there seems to have been domestic accommodation for the family, whilst another floor was used to store wool.

The mill was replaced in stages over the next fifty or sixty years, though it remained primarily water-powered, the steam engine being used just when water levels were low. In the early days, the manufacturers put much of the weaving work out to cottage workers in the district but by the 1850s the majority of the work was mill-based, and the mill was almost fully steam-powered, though water-power continued to be used in a small way right up to the twentieth century.

The mill had been built on land held by Benjamin Gartside in 1790 in the manor of Wakefield, but the Gartsides do not seem to have manufactured there. It may have been built 'speculatively' by Benjamin Gartside, that is, he built the mill and let it out to clothiers. The land was owned or leased by a tanner called Benjamin Green and it was his daughter, Mary, who married Ben Gartside.

The Land Tax returns of Austonley[9] show that, although Benjamin Gartside owned the mill, it was occupied by John Kenion. His widow stayed on in the domestic area of the mill and is probably the Ellen Kenyon who is mentioned as living in the mill in the 1804 insurance papers.

In 1797 the mill appears to have been called Field End Mill and was built three storeys high, covering about 70ft by 24ft (21 × 7m). The ground floor was in two parts, each with its own external door and water-wheel, whilst the first floor contained an 'ingen chamber' [engine chamber], three double and one single scribbling engines and a 40-spindle billy.

The first floor was also used as a dwelling-house with a fireplace. The second floor also had a fireplace, but was used as a wool chamber. It was insured for £1,800, which was a considerable sum of money in those days.

By 1800, Holmbridge Mill was let to Joshua Barber, a wool scribbler of Holmbridge, and two years later was in use by Joshua and Joseph Barber. The Barber family seem to have had considerable interests in this area, being primarily farmers but producing cloth as well.

Various branches of the family were in different mill buildings at times. One member of the family – Henry Barber – spent some time in Derbyshire, where he married and his first two sons, Joseph and John, were born. His third son, George, was born back in Cartworth. The rest of the extensive Barber family seem to have stayed in the Holmfirth area throughout their lives.

The Factory Commission Inquiry

The 1833 Factory Commission inquiry describes the mill as being used for scribbling, carding, slubbing wool and milling or fulling cloth. There were still two water-wheels, together with a 14hp steam engine 'only used in cases of extreme drought or scarcity of water'. Joseph Barber & Co manufactured their own cloth but also finished cloth for other firms on commission.

Only 27 people were employed at the time, but five of those were under 10 years of age, eight were aged 10–12, and five were 12–14 years old. The children under 12 all earned 4s. 6d. (22½p) a week.

Days began at 6 am and finished at 8 at night, with a half-hour break at 8 am for breakfast, an hour for dinner at noon, and half an hour for a drink at 4.30 pm. The report comments that working hours were fewer in the winter than in the summer. This was not, as we might expect, because of the shorter days or the difficulty of working in the cold, but because of a decrease in demand during the winter. Employees worked a six-day week, but for two hours less on a Saturday. There were no paid holidays.

According to Joseph Barber & Co, 'no corporal punishment is sanctioned' but this belies the testimony of many of the children themselves, at least in other mills. The masters may have thought there was no physical punishment in their mill, but they were not often in the mill itself – it was too dirty and dusty.

The firm also stated that 'we are decidedly of the opinion that there should be some restriction as to the hours of labour performed by children', yet they continued to employ them for 12 hours a day, 70 hours a week. It may have been even longer, since the statements made by other children suggest that meal breaks were by no means as long in practice as the masters told the Commission they were.

Samuel Looke, who worked at a mill in Holmfirth, stated that he finished work 'at dark' – sometimes as late as 10 pm – with no break apart from a mere half-hour for lunch; and, for the first six months of working, the children worked for nothing as they were considered to be 'training' and therefore not worth paying. After all this, the children still went to Sunday School in an effort to learn to read and write.

Nowadays it is difficult to understand the attitude of many of the mill owners. They worked children for over 70 hours a week in appalling conditions, yet they were staunch churchgoers. Joseph Barber was one of the trustees of Holmfirth Methodist Chapel and no doubt considered himself a 'God-fearing' man.

The mill buildings were gradually extended at the south end, along with some free-standing buildings and various improvements, including by 1840 an engine-house, wool store, dam and stable. The Austenley township valuation of 1843 shows the mill valued at £195 7s. (£195.35), with a further £80 value added after 'improvements'. The stable block was valued at only 18s. (90p).

Fifteen years later, the rateable value was shown separately as:

Mill	£125 9 shillings (£125.45)
Warehouse	£7 18 shillings (£7.90)
Dyehouse, Warehouse, stables etc	£23 12 shillings (£23.60)
Total	£156 19 shillings (£156.95)

The rateable value was also reduced in 1862 to £125 9s. (£125.45). Whether this reflects the reduced value of the local rates, political views on business rates or some problems with the mill buildings is not known.

Barber Brothers

Typically for this era, before the Married Women's Property Act of 1893, ownership of the mill had passed from Firth Gartside to his brothers-in-law (not his sisters) – Joshua Charlesworth, John Wood, Richard Hinchliffe and John Barber. It was Barber who had married Firth's sister, Fanny Gartside, thus linking the two families.

In 1860 the four Barber brothers – John (Fanny's husband), Edmund, Joseph and Joshua junior – leased the mill for ten years at £350 per annum. This lease included the fittings of 'waterwheels, steam engine, stocks, shafting and going gear' to a value of £700. More land was bought in Holmbridge, on the far bank of the River Holme, and the Barbers built new weaving sheds there, which were fully steam-powered by 1859. These buildings were joined to become Clarence Mill, which is still standing.

The brothers continued in Holmbridge Mill, taking ten-year leases, and were still there when the River Pollution Commission investigated the area in 1871. The firm told the commission that they employed 150 people, producing 150,000lb weight (68 tonnes) of goods each year with a value of £30,000. This was dyed, not bleached – the implication being that they were not causing any pollution because they did not use bleach.

The firm told the commission that 'the bed of the stream has not silted up opposite our works' but they also said that 'the whole of the waste liquid produced at our works, except soapsuds, flows direct into the stream'. They went on to list some of the chemicals and dyestuffs used in the course of a year:

> 35,840lb [16.3 tonnes] of logwood (a wood of a dark red colour, used for dyeing)
> 448lb [203kg] of argol (used to make cream of tartar)
> 672lb [305kg] of madder (plant whose roots are used to make a red dye)
> 1,008lb [457kg] of bichrome (a mordaunt used to fix the dyes)
> 244lb [111kg] of fustic (tropical American tree from which a yellow dye was made)
> 224lb [102kg] of barwood (produced a reddish brown colour)

Clarence Mill, Holmebridge.

2oolb [91kg] of alum (alkali used in the scouring process)
20 tons of olive oil
8,960lb [4.06 tonnes] of soap
17,920lb [8.1 tonnes] of alkali
800 gallons [3,500 litres] urine (used in the scouring process to neutralise the soap)

Both waste wool and 'the excrements of our workpeople' were used for manure on the land. The stream may not have silted up, but it cannot have smelt very nice!

When Joseph died in 1880, Edmund and Joshua paid £591 for the value of his share in the mill. John died in 1882, followed the next year by Edmund, whose estate was valued at £3,923 9s. 6d. (£3,923.47½). The weaving sheds were later sold for £725 to James Hirst of Lockwood, who sold them the following year to J B Norcliffe for £750.

By 1890 William Henry, eldest son of Joshua Barber, and his cousin John Barber were able to buy back the mills from Norcliffe's widow for a total of £920 and the firm continued working from the site, with the further purchase of the buildings on the far side of the River Holme in 1900.

W H & J Barber Ltd

The firm made fancy worsted suitings, and trouserings. They were one of the first to have a telephone in the area – number Holmfirth 2 – and opened a warehouse in Huddersfield at 6 Britannia Chambers in St George's Square, right in the centre of town and close to the railway for easy transport of their finished cloths all over the country.

Unfortunately, some years after the formation of the partnership, John Barber was killed in a car accident, leaving the running of the mill to William Henry Barber.

With expanding trade at the beginning of the twentieth century, extra looms were bought, with a loom width of 90 inches (2.3m), and a new engine–house and boiler–house were built for the Pollitt & Wigzell steam engine. This was replaced in 1937 by a second–hand engine by Clayton & Goodfellows of Blackburn.

Letterhead of W H & J Barber.

Worsted & Woollen Manufacturers   LIMITED

HOLMBRIDGE, near Huddersfield, England

All Communications to be addressed to the Mills

—— *SPECIALITIES :* ——

Fancy Worsteds and Woollens Suitings and Trouserings

Orders executed direct by Cash Payment against Bill of Lading, or through the usual buying channels. Samples sent to responsible Buyers with reference. Please send copy of order when buying through Merchants.

FABRICANTS D'ETOFFES DE PEIGNÉS ET DE LAINAGES.	FABRICANTES DE LANAS Y ESTAMBRES.	FABBRICANTI DI LANE E FILATI.	製造絲錦反呢布 特貨
Spécialités : Etoffas fantaisie de peignés et lainages. Etoffes pour complets et pantalons.	Especialidades : Estambres y Lanas de Fantasia. Telas para Trajes y para Cortes de Pantalones.	Specialità Lane e Filati di Fantasia Stoffe per Abiti e pantaloni.	袴衣毛花 布料料樣 料 絲 錦 呢

The firm had always been woollen manufacturers, preparing and spinning the yarn, loading the yarn onto carts and trundling them down the tunnel that ran under the roadway between the mill buildings. Once woven, the cloth would be brought back to the larger mill for wet scouring. The smaller mill was also used for dry finishing, warehousing and packing.

However, woollen cloth was the lower end of the market in price; for the firm to survive, improvements had to be made. They gradually changed to manufacturing mainly worsted. The plan of the mill shows the use of some of the buildings about 1950.

Workers mainly lived nearby, as Mr Barber explained: 'We always advertised that preference would be given to those living in the area, since they tended to stay longer. Training is an expensive business, so we wanted our workers to stay with us. When we finally had to close, many had been with us for years.'

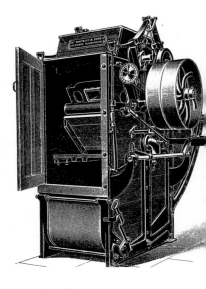

An early milling and scouring machine.

In 1923 William Henry died and was buried in Holmbridge church, near the grave of his cousin. The firm was taken over by his son Maurice, who was able to visit South America for a year, making contacts and gaining the firm a lot of business. By this time 100% of the manufacture was for export.

However, by the 1950s, South American trade had ended because of tariffs, so new markets had to found in Egypt and Middle East, Canada and the USA. Trade was good at this time and the firm bought the name and goodwill of Benjamin Vickerman & Co from Taylor Hill Mills.

The mending room at Holmbridge Mill about 1970.

olmbridge Mill

Sketch plan dated about 1960.

Key	
1	Old mill
3	Waterwheel house
4	Engine house
5	Blacksmith's shop
6	Dyehouse until 1951 when it became the engine house
7	Tentering room and stove
8	Yarn Store
9	Two cottages
10	Weaving shed
11	Weaving shed
12	Offices
13	Pattern room
14	Store room
15	Engine house and boiler
16	Worsted spinning mill
16B	Toilets
17 and 18 – part of Holmebridge Dyeworks which were the earlier mill. Used for storage and some scribbling just before the Second World War.	

Barber grave.

Trade expanded to the Far East, Hong Kong, New Zealand and Australia, until Australia and New Zealand introduced a 120% tariff, which closed the market. By the 1960s, the Middle East trade had ended too.

However, there was still trade with Far East, especially Japan. Special designs were needed for each market and Barbers had to keep an eye on prices. 'I worked out the cost of buying a suit in both England and Japan,' Mr Barber said, 'and when the cost of a suit in Japan equalled the cost of buying a Mini car in England, I knew the writing was on the wall.'

The firm decided to take advantage of government support, with severance pay to ensure workers got a good pay-out, and went into voluntary liquidation in 1975. The mill was sold off, the oldest parts being demolished in 1994.

The start of the demolition, 1994.

Newsome Mill

In July 1823,[10] John Taylor married Betty Dyson in Newsome Church. As Betty was the daughter of a wealthy local businessman, Joseph Dyson, the wedding was quite a grand affair, with the first 'shays' or chaises being seen in the area. Three years later, John began building Croft House, which was to be his family home for many years.

Ordnance Survey map 1907: scale 25″ to 1 mile.

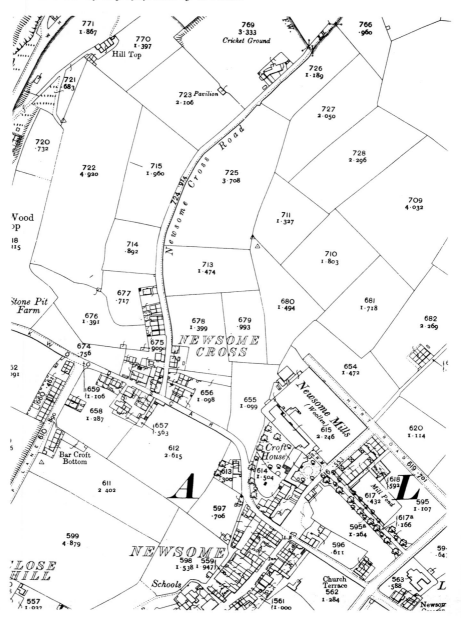

Since John was the son of Charles Taylor, a cloth manufacturer at Almondbury Common, it is not surprising that in 1827 he was establishing a business for himself in Newsome. He built some sheds near his new house and began the production of patterned fabrics using the new 'Witch' loom, which enabled weavers to weave flower patterns on cloth for waistcoating.

Cloth was still sent to Almondbury Common for finishing at this time but in just five years he had completed the long chimney needed for the engine and in 1837 a new warehouse was erected. This building was often used for religious meetings, since it was one of the largest buildings in the area.

In 1840 the first dyehouse was erected and by 1843 the firm was already exporting to South America. One document shows cloth being taken across to Montevideo, Buenos Aires, Valparaiso and Lima, where sales were made at each port.

The dyehouse had been erected near two reservoirs, but water had to be purchased at great expense from Huddersfield Corporation. Taylor

Ornate entrance way with datestone.

eventually bought property at Spring Wood to supply water for the mill. In very dry weather, horses would be used to bring great barrels full of water to the mill.

Ten years later, trouserings were being manufactured, providing employment for outworkers, though an 1853 trade directory[11] lists the business as John Taylor & Sons, shawl manufacturers. In 1855, John William and Henry Beaumont Taylor took over the Colne Road Mills whilst Fred and Joseph Walter Taylor continued at Newsome.

However, tragedy struck in 1865. Joseph Walter was killed in an accident, when he fell from a ladder in the mill. Fred then went into partnership with Joah Lodge to form the firm of Taylor & Lodge.

The partnership lasted only a few years but was not without excitement. In the early hours of a quiet Sunday in July 1872[12] the mill caught fire and the alarm was raised. At that time the local police were expected to act as firemen, as well as the fire crews provided by businesses. The local constable, PC Worsnop, informed his boss, Mr Withers. He in turn told Inspector Galvin, who ordered out thirty constables under the command of Sergeant Fox.

The fire brigade from John Brooke's at Armitage Bridge arrived, as did the Huddersfield Corporation Brigade and crews from Kaye's Executors and the Liverpool, London and Globe Insurance Co, who insured the mill.

The roof of the building soon fell in, and the concern was to stop the fire spreading to the warehouse nearby. Such was the heat that the windows of the warehouse melted and the cloth inside was scorched, but after 'great exertion' by all the firefighters the fire was brought under control. Over £10,000 of damage had been done, including machinery and cloth.

The employers and the workers were often actively involved in fighting the fire. Fred Taylor was at the scene; when the wall at the western end of the mill finally fell down, he narrowly escaped serious injury.

A fire of this size normally meant that employees would be out of work, with no unemployment pay. In this case, though, Taylor & Lodge announced that they intended to rent looms at other premises in order to keep production going until their own building was back in use. Shortly afterwards the partnership ended, though Joah Lodge went on to found a new firm called Taylor & Lodge, which still exists.

In 1873, Ephraim Beaumont Taylor bought Newsome Mills from Fred Taylor, who died in 1874, and went into partnership with Joshua Littlewood.

Gas

In 1873, as part of the rebuilding, some modernisation took place and local people were invited to view it.

A short time ago we gave a description of a new patent apparatus for making air gas. On Wednesday night we had the opportunity of witnessing a large apparatus in use at the works of Messrs Taylor & Littlewood's Newsome Mills. The apparatus had been fixed by Mr Joel Jepson, ironmonger, New Street, the sole agent for Yorkshire Air Gas Light Company Limited in the weaving shed, and there were about 200 burners in use on Wednesday night in the weaving shed and spinning room.

The pipes formerly used for coal gas, with which the place used to be lighted, were brought into requisition for this air gas. The light was steady and clear, and there was smaller amount of flame composed of that dark colour which gives no light than is usual with the ordinary coal gas; and from what we saw we are convinced that when the apparatus is got into thoroughly working order (which it was not last night, the cistern not having been then fixed so as to supply the generator with gasogen regularly) it will produce a light far superior to that usually obtained from ordinary coal gas.

The apparatus occupied a very small space, there is no danger of explosion, the gas does not smell offensive nor does it corrode the pipes and what is of great importance the gas can be made for about 2 shillings and sixpence per 1000 foot [12½p per 28.3 cu. m] which will not burn out as rapidly as 1000 [cu.] foot of ordinary gas. The great purity of the gas too, renders it valuable for lighting rooms expensive decorated or furnished or containing valuable pictures.[13]

Internal construction with fireproof columns.

However, the claim of its superiority was short-lived. Less than a year later, the paper ran the story of a 'Serious Gas Explosion' at the mills. Some of the gas was made on the mill premises by the firm itself but, when this ran out, gas was bought from the Huddersfield Corporation gas works. In order to swap over, the equipment had to be emptied of water and the nightwatchman had to go down to see if all the water was out.

Unfortunately, he took a lamp down with him, which wasn't a good idea, causing the explosion and 'blowing the gasometer clean out of the water-hold and smashing into pieces the three pillars used for suspending the gasometer'.[14] The man's thigh was broken, but all the others working around the gasometer at the time escaped injury.

Spiral staircase.

The building itself was stone with iron columns, to help cut down the risks from fire, but the floors were wood, with grooves where the spinning mules ran back and forth. A narrow, iron spiral-staircase ran from top to bottom of the mill, with sets of toilets squashed under the iron steps on each floor. It was only later that separate men's and women's toilets were installed.

The 1870s

In 1875 Joshua Littlewood, Ephraim's partner, moved into Croft House, where his youngest daughter Ruth was born. Joshua – born in Deanhouse, Honley – had worked with his father, Hiram, a woollen manufacturer, for some years before joining John Taylor and Co as a designer at Colne Mills. He then moved to Newsome and eventually became a partner in the firm.

After the 1872 fire, the buildings were rebuilt within a short time and in 1876 the firm were advertising for tenders for new weaving sheds.[15] By 1885 a new, four-storey mill was planned, adjoining the weaving shed and including a dining room for 500 workpeople. It was described as a 'Splendid block of buildings, mills and weaving sheds of great extent and admirable arrangement'.

All processes, from dealing with raw wool to cloth manufacturing, were being carried out at Newsome Mill at this time. The business had over 10,000 spindles and 200 looms, with 600 people making fancy worsteds, trousering, coating and woollen goods.

Some of the first employees included John Hawkyard, William Wilkinson, James Dawson, and the husband-and-wife team of William and Sarah (or Sally) Crossley. For many years, Sally was the only female weaver in the mill. The book-keeper was William Clelland, who had come down from Scotland, married a local girl and stayed to become the mill's manager.

About this time the mill whistle was introduced, to ensure workers arrived on time. At 6 am promptly, the gates were shut and anyone who did not get to the mill

Newsome Mill.

by that time would lose a day's work – and a day's pay. The whistle continued for many years but eventually 'The last war put an end to the shrill mill hooter from Taylor & Littlewood which used to awaken the good people of Newsome from their slumbers to summon the workforce to the mill.'[16] Many people must have been glad of the silence.

The business won the gold medal at the Paris Exhibition of 1878 for fancy cloths and first prize at the Sydney Exhibition of 1879 for the same class of goods. Much of the manufacturing was for export and the firm had agencies in Glasgow, Paris, New York and Melbourne.

During the 1870s, the textile trade was expanding, though wages were kept low. This was in a long period of deflation, when most wages and prices dropped, at least slightly. By 1873, Taylor & Littlewood were paying about £1 10/- (£1.50) a week to pattern weavers.[17] It is hard to tell whether these increased earnings resulted simply from the efficiency of working from standard designs.

Six years later, Thomas Halstead, described as a pattern weaver and designer, was being paid £3 a week, whilst his son, Alfred, was earning £2. James Maffin, in the same department, was paid only £1 4/- (£1.20). Two youngsters, Sam Eastwood and Elizabeth Dawson, were paid 7/- (35p) and 11/- (55p) respectively and were presumably trainees.

In 1873 the Cloth Pressers' Society produced a survey of average pay in thirty firms in the area.[18] Some firms paid by piece rate, others by the day. The day-rate average was £1 4s. 10d. (£1.24) per week, though some hands were earning as much as £1 12s. (£1.60), so Taylor & Littlewood seem to have been paying the 'going rate' for textile work.

Over the years, the nature of work at the mill seems to have changed. In 1879 jobs included slay makers and heald knitters, stockinette winders and weavers, and wool sorters. None of these jobs was listed in the 1902 wage book, but combing, drawing, twisting and worsted spinning had been added.

Numbers employed changed over the years too. In 1879 there were only 23 menders, increasing to 51 in 1902 and 114 by 1923. With the decline in the textile trade, the numbers had decreased to 48 by 1954. Mending was the one job that could easily be undertaken by women at home whilst they had young children, but even in the mill this job was always done by women.

Menders were highly skilled, but they were still not paid a man's wage. Their wage was about 15/- per week in 1879, slipping (with deflation) to 14/9 in 1886. By 1923 it ranged from £2 to £4, and was typically £5 to £6 by 1954. As this was generally paid on piece rate, it is difficult to be sure how much they generally earned – some worked harder than others, some spent more time on the work.

The warpers were paid a similar amount to the menders in 1879, but by 1954 their pay had increased to £7 to £9 per week for women and about £10 for men.

Tuners, who kept the machines running, saw their wages increase from £1–2 a week in 1879 to about £10 a week in 1954. That was a high wage at that time and worsted spinners seem to have done even better. Those employed in 1902 were paid about 8/- (40p) per week, yet could earn up to £14 per week in 1954. Obviously, the amounts paid included overtime, which meant hard work to reach the top rates.

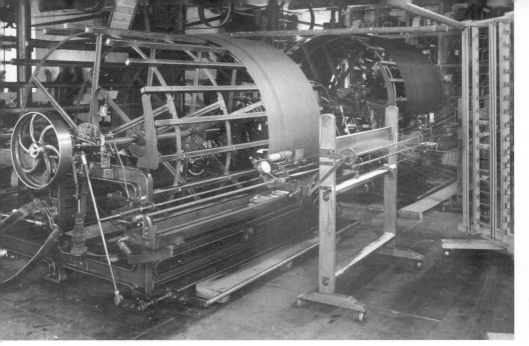

Preparing the warp on a warping mill.

The cloths were men's suitings – pin stripes, grey background, tiny dogtooth checks and herringbone in fawn, purple, navy or brown.[19] The exact pattern depended on the customers' requirements and had to be changed according to the season – fashion is no new invention.

The pattern books contain clippings from the orders, showing the variety of weaves possible. Each order includes the pattern number, the number of pieces required, a cutting of the pattern to ensure accuracy, its price, the length and width required and the weight per yard.

Nothing was left to chance and there was much correspondence about the quality expected and delivered, exact colours and so on. Some firms required their own 'copyright' patterns. In 1919 Thomas Cresswell & Co of Huddersfield ordered two pieces of suiting 'to be absolutely confined to us' and made from all combed wool. Taylor & Littlewood had a high reputation and even had orders from J & J Minnis of Savile Row in London.

Like all buildings, the mill required constant maintenance. B Graham & Nephew carried out extensive repairs and building work over many years, including masonry work. They also flagged the yard, presumably because otherwise the constant coming and going of wagons would have churned up so much mud. It was also probably for this reason that the firm had to contribute to the cost of 'making' Hart Street outside the mill itself.

In 1883 B Graham & Nephew were working on the dyehouse and a new tank, and providing a new drying-room over No 3 boiler at a cost of more than £275. C C Donkersley & Co charged £11 for iron girders over the drying machine.

The following year a new Shiel boiler of 30 × 8ft (27 × 7m) was bought from Joseph Adamson & Co at a cost of £322. This included an allowance of £150 for the old boiler, which was taken in exchange. Grahams installed it and renewed the masonry around the new boiler.

Masters and Workers

It is interesting to contrast the life-styles of master and servants. Most mill workers lived nearby, as did Joshua Littlewood and Ephraim Beaumont Taylor. That was about the only similarity.

David Ainley was a presser and finisher, preparing finished cloth for sale and delivery to customers. In 1881 he was 55 years old, living in Ing Lane just down the hill from Newsome Mill and earning £1 1/- (£1.05) per week. His daughter Clara also worked for the firm, earning just 13s. (65p) as a mender.

In the same lane lived the Crow family – Thomas was a joiner earning £1 18s. 3d. (£1.91), on which he had to support his wife and three young boys – and the Rothwell family – Henry was employed as a worsted reed maker, earning £1 10/- (£1.50) a week.

Like many others, all the Mace family worked in the woollen industry. John at 54 was a beamer, earning £1 1s. 8d. (£1.08); his son James, aged 16, worked alongside him earning just 7s. (35p) a week, whilst his daughter Amelia was employed as a stockinette winder and earned the grand total of 10s. (50p), though she was only 15 years old.

A pressing machine.

In contrast, the records show that in less than a year E B Taylor, one of the mill owners, spent over £410 just on building work in the billiard room. It had a slate roof, a solid mahogany mantelpiece over the fireplace and a chandelier, and there was mosaic floor to the lavatory nearby. This was before purchase of the billiard table, chairs or any other furniture, and decorating the room. He spent more on this one room than the above employees earned between them in a year.

Treats

Despite the expenses of running the mill, in 1877 E B Taylor paid for a treat for the old folk, with tea at the Fountains Inn. Eighty people sat down for the meal and John Dews, the oldest, proposed the toast, saying 'he'd known the firm since it started 50 years ago'. The Newsome Brass Band played to entertain the party.[20]

Just as in other mills, there were not just regular treats for the workpeople but also 'extra' treats to celebrate special events. One such occurred in June 1866 when F N Taylor, a member of the firm, got married. A hundred hands and a few friends were taken to Hollingworth Lake near Manchester 'in waggonnettes, buses etc'[21] by way of Elland, Sowerby Bridge, Ripponden and Littleborough.

On arrival there was boating, dancing, bowling and billiards for those who didn't want to venture outside. At 4 pm a 'substantial and well laid out knife and fork tea' was served and followed by the usual speeches and toasts. They must have returned to Huddersfield at quite a late hour. Such outings were only possible during the summer months when days were long.

Twentieth Century

Taylor & Littlewood were one of the first businesses to install a telephone system, their number being Huddersfield 198. Telegrams could be sent to 'Breezy Huddersfield' – Newsome Mill is at the top of the hill, its clock tower being a landmark for the area.

The twentieth century was a time of alternate expansion and decline. In 1914–18, the mills were working at full capacity, with 140 looms in use up to 1930. This number dropped slightly to 100, and again just after the Second World War, when it fell to 80. There was a slight increase up to the 1970s.

In 1977 the firm celebrated its 150th anniversary amid the prevailing export boom. There was an official lunch and mill tour for a number of civic and wool textile dignitaries, together with a social get-together for past and present employees. It was said to be the 'oldest privately owned fine worsted manufacturing company in Huddersfield with their own weaving and spinning plants.'[22]

After a report of this anniversary appeared, a customer asked if it was possible to reproduce the cloths manufactured in the early 1800s, shown in the company's pattern books. It was, and the exclusive designs were produced, 'an unusual proof of Taylor & Littlewood's ability to meet a customer's individual requirements.'[23]

Also in 1977, new Jacquard machinery was fitted to some of the Dornier shuttleless weaving machines that had been purchased. By 'textile

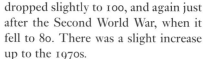

Newsome Clock Tower.

Taylor & Littlewood Ltd.

High-class WORSTED MANUFACTURERS

All Communications to be addressed
to Head Office and Mills.

High-class Fancy Suitings, Trouserings and Overcoatings, Covert Coatings, Bedford Cords, Riding Tweeds, Motor Cloths and Plain Coatings

Newsome Mills, **HUDDERSFIELD,** - *England*

LONDON: 5 GOLDEN SQUARE, W.

Orders executed direct by Cash Payment against Bill of Lading, or through the usual buying channels.
Samples sent to responsible Buyers with reference. Please send copy of order when buying through Merchants.

Etoffes Fantaisie de premier choix pour Complets, Pantalons et Pardessus. Etoffes pour paletots, Velours à côtes Bedford, Casimirs pour l'équitation. Etoffes d'automobiles et Draps unis pour paletots.

Commandes exécutées directement contre payement au comptant contre connaissement ou par les intermédiaires habituels. Echantillons envoyés à tout acheteur établi muni de références. Prière de nous adresser duplicata de toute commande faite par l'entremise d'exportateurs.

Géneros de Fantasia de primera calidad para trajes, cortes de pantalón y gabanes, Chaquetas y Sobretodos. Pana Bedford para refuerzos. Paño de lana de dos colores para Equitación. Géneros para automóviles y paños lisos para Chaquetas.

Los pedidos se ejecutan directamente mediante pago al contado contra conocimientos de embarque o por los medios comerciales de costumbre. Se envían muestras a compradores de responsabilidad que den referencias. Al hacer pedidos por medio de comerciantes envíese copia de las notas de pedido.

Stoffe Fantasia Prima Qualità per Costumi, Pantaloni & Cappotti. Stoffe per Copri tutto Bedford, Casimir per Equitazione. Stoffe per Automobili & panni uniti.

Si eseguiscono gli ordini direttamente per pagamento contanti contro Polizza di carico oppure per tramite delle solite vie d'acquisto. Si spediscono campioni a Compratori terii con riferenze. Si prega voler trasmettere copia dell'ordine passando delle ordinazioni per tramite di negozianti.

上等花品衣料、袴及大衣料。
花品及素衣料。
游行之布料、
騎馬的、土維特布料。
口為土、布料、比德樞、繩布。

Letterhead of Taylor & Littlewood Ltd.

week' – the July holidays – in 1978, workers were looking forward with confidence. There were full order books and 99 per cent of the business was for export, with orders from Hong Kong, Japan, the Middle East, Europe and the USA.

It came as a considerable shock when in November the firm introduced short-time working, which they insisted would only affect a minimal number of workers, but by 1980 sixty were made redundant when the spinning plant closed. Taylor & Littlewood had been innovative in introducing the new Dobcross looms into their mills in 1895 but now these were sold off.

In 1981, production began to run down because of poor trading conditions worldwide. The union (NUDBTW) were said to be deeply saddened as they considered Taylor & Littlewood to be a 'good firm' – 'no firm could have tried harder to keep abreast of technological progress and remain competitive.'[24]

In September 1981, forty more jobs were lost, though the trade names continued to be marketed by a firm in Leeds. Newsome Mills became simply a design and marketing base, with a small weaving operation to prepare new design ranges before production. It was a little ironical that the following year the company won the 'townwear' prize in a competition run by the National Wool Textile Export Corporation.

In 1983, most of the remaining jobs were lost and the following year the mill site was bought by Huddersfield Estate Company and formed into units to be leased to smaller firms. The 1986 Yorkshire and Lancashire Textile Industry Directory lists English Oak (Woollen) Ltd, who were a 'consultant designing, commission pattern weaving and warping' business. Also in the mill complex was Texpak (Yorkshire) Ltd, who offered a warehousing service that covered 'examining, sealing, transferring, rolling, rigging, wrapping and packing of worsted piece goods'.

As the mill chimney ceased to be used, it eventually had to be demolished and this 150ft (45.7m) landmark was taken down 'brick by brick'.[25]

Dobcross Weaving, one of the firms in the Newsome Mills units, found fame in 1997 when some of its cloth was used to make the midnight blue tuxedo that Pierce Brosnan wore as 007 in *Tomorrow Never Dies*. The cloth had been designed by English Oak, who are also in Newsome Mills.

Other Mills in the Area

Austonley township

Bilberry Mill	This mill was damaged in the 1852 Holmfirth flood, but by 1857 Joshua Barber & Co were renting rooms. In the 1870s it was used by Thomas Hirst & Sons and known as Hirst's mill. F H McGrath had moved here by 1910.
Black Sike Mill	Built at the end of the eighteenth century as a three-storey scribbling mill. In 1861 T Barber & Co were treating their workers from this mill to the usual hearty supper. The evening concluded with a rendition of the National Anthem 'in most glorious discord', the *Chronicle* said.[26]
Bottoms Mill	FCR 1834 lists J Harpin & Co as occupiers. Joseph Barber was here in 1873, when he went bankrupt. By 1910, T & J Tinker were here with J Throstle Barber, stockinette and fancy weaver.
Digley Mill	FCR 1834 shows G & J Hirst in the mill. This became George Hirst & Co by 1857. Joseph Greenwood & Sons ran the mills from *c*.1881 into the twentieth century. Now demolished and under the Digley Reservoir.
Yew Tree Mills	The firm of Butterworth & Roberts began here in the 1860s and are still operating from this mill.

Brockholes township

Rock Mill
A three-storey mill, built *c.*1860, it was the cotton factory of Turner & Bower. Joseph Sykes & Co, woollen & worsted manufacturers, were there from the 1880s. It was demolished in 1974.

Cartworth township

Dover Mill
Built *c.*1830, this was used by J Bower & Co at the end of nineteenth century. By 1950, H Turner had moved in.

Green Lane Mill
FCR 1834 shows Hinchliffe & Taylor in this mill, built *c.*1800. In 1875 the business was sold off.[27] By 1910 Bower & Sons Ltd were operating here.

New Fold Mill
This appears on an 1854 map but little is known about this woollen mill.

Perseverance Mill
Sometimes referred to as Dyson's mill, it was built *c.*1820. FCR 1834 shows Messrs Roberts & Sandford here. Jonathan Sandford and some of his family perished in the 1852 Holmfirth flood. Walter Greenwood & Sons seem to have been using the mill in 1910.

Ribbleden Mill
A mid-nineteenth-century mill used by Lawton & Co in 1910s

Swan Bank Mill
FCR 1834 says this was built in 1825. Hinchliffe & Horncastle were using the mill in the mid-nineteenth century; in 1910, John Beever & Sons, hearth rug manufacturer.

Washpit Mill
A water-powered mill built in the 1830s expanded to include steam power *c.*1850. In 1841 Hinchliffe Bros were leasing part of this mill. They were followed by J B Watkinson & Son, who remained many years. The mill was later taken by Westwood Yarns Ltd.

Fulstone township

Moorbrook Mill
Bought by Moorhouse & Brook in 1910 to manufacture woollen & worsted cloth; this firm remained in business until recently.

Sude Hill Mill
This mill was involved in the Plug Riots in the 1840s. It was taken over in the 1860s by George Booth & Co, who became Booth, Pitt & Co, and then William Pitt & Co by 1890. Fred Lawton & Co were here in 1910. Now industrial units, some associated with textiles.

Hepworth township

Dobroyd Mill
A mid-nineteenth century mill, where Jonathan Thorpe & Sons made woollen and worsted cloth before 1914. Now J T Knitting Ltd and John Woodhead (Dobroyd Mills) Ltd occupy industrial units here.

Moorbrook Mill.

Holme township
Brownhill Mill   This mill housed a variety of firms throughout its life.
Rake Mill   FCR 1834 lists this mill, used by William & Edward Leake in 1836. In 1915 it housed a turbine generating electricity for the village.

Holmfirth township
Tom Mills   Shown on an 1854 map, near the bridge in Holmfirth.
Albert Mills   B Mellor & Sons, dyers and fullers, were here to c.1950.
Bank End Mill   A water-powered fulling mill, occupied by J Roebuck & Sons according to FCR 1834. It was for sale in 1855.
Hinchcliffe Mill   This is an example of an early fulling mill around which a village grew. Charlesworth & Butterworth were here in the mid-nineteenth century. They became Butterworth & Roberts about the 1890s. The mill was gutted by fire in 1901, but partly rebuilt and leased to Whiteley & Green; by 1910 it was used by Weavetec commission weavers.
Riverside Mill   When in 1894 the Yorkshire Felting Company went into liquidation, this later mill was taken over by Allen Hinchliffe & Sons, shoddy & mungo.

Victoria Mill	Built in 1848, it was occupied for many years by Thomas Hinchliffe & Sons. Clough Bros, woollen and worsted manufacturers, were in the mill in 1950. By 1979 it was the home of VM Fabrications, a sheet-metal company.

Honley township

Cocking Steps Mill	Built *c.*1760 as a fulling mill, it was then used for manufacturing by the Wrigley family. By 1950 the Netherton Spinning Co Ltd had taken over. It has now been converted to private dwellings.
Crossley Mill	William Brook rented this mill on the Dartmouth estate *c.*1738. William's family had been associated with textiles since the sixteenth century; he was one of the first to use steam power in the area. His son, John, expanded the mills, but in 1819 he moved to Armitage Bridge Mills (q.v.), forming John Brooke & Sons. FCR 1834 shows D Shaw & Co here, hence its name Shaw's Factory. By 1900 it housed Allen Thornton & Sons.
Dean House Mill	This fulling and scribbling mill of the 1790s was occupied by Nathaniel and Godfrey Berry, who went bankrupt in 1800. The son of Hiram Littlewood (see Newsome Mills) was involved in an accident at this mill. In 1910 it was used by Thomas Dyson & Sons.
Grove Mill	Originally a stone-built sawmill, it was used by a brewer, as a corn mill by Edward Robertshaw and then, for many years from the end of the nineteenth century, for wool/worsted by Littlewood & Co, stovers & finishers.
Honley Mill	On maps of the 1770s this was a corn and scribbling mill on the Dartmouth estates. Messrs Hinchliffe & Heap leased the mill, this firm being taken over by Hinchliffe Brothers in the mid-nineteenth century.
Lord's Mill	Also known as Wood Bottom Mill, in 1805 this scribbling and fulling mill on the Dartmouth estates was used by John & George Beaumont. In the 1850s Heap Brothers leased the mill. This firm later became Heap & Walker.
Neiley Mill	See Crossley Mill.
Old Moll Mill	See Thirstin Mill.
Reins Mill	Built in 1847, it was used by Charles Dean & Sons at the end of the nineteenth century. David France & Co were there at the turn of the century, but by 1950 it housed Marsden Sykes & Co and N Marsh Ltd.
Shaw's Factory	See Crossley Mill.
Smithy Place Mill	Built *c.*1789 by Giles Gartside, dyer, by 1816 the mill was occupied by Firth Gartside (see Holmbridge Mills). FCR 1834

shows Joshua Robinson in the mill and the Robinson family remained here for many years.

Thirstin Mill	Built *c.*1790, this mill was recorded by FCR 1834 as run by Tom Hinchliffe. Eastwood Brothers took it over *c.*1890 and were still there in 1910. Old Moll Mill was also on this site and both were up for sale in 1859.[28]
Victoria Mills	Built *c.*1845, it was occupied by Beaumont & Stocks. YTD 1910 shows T H Sykes & Co.
Wood Bottom Mill	See Lord's Mill.
Wrigley's Mill	See Cocking Steps Mill.

Lockwood township

Bath Mill	Built *c.*1850, this mill was used by Joah Lodge & Sons by the 1880s, then by Allen Priest & Sons in 1910 and up to 1970s.
Britannia Mill, Stoney Battery	Started as a four-storey woollen mill *c.*1835, it was rebuilt in 1861 by John Firth & Sons and then leased to various firms. John Crowther & Sons were here in 1865. When they moved to Bank Bottom Mill, Marsden, Britannia Mill Co Ltd took over. It is now used by Bradbury & Co.
Broadfield Mill	Godfrey Berry moved here from Folly Hall *c.*1850 to form Messrs Berry & Crowther; this became Henry Crowther & Sons. In 1897 Kaye & Stewart took over the mills.

Britannia Mill, Stoney Battery.

Crosland Moor Bottom Mill	Built about the 1840s by Crosland & Sons; the eldest son was T P Crosland, who was MP for Huddersfield. The mill burnt down in 1992.
Dungeon Mill	See Park Valley Mills.
Firth's Mill	See Britannia Mills, Lockwood.
Lockwood Mills	Built *c.* 1847 by George Crosland on the site of an earlier mill. Nicholl & Pratt, dyers, operated from here in 1950.
Park Valley Mill	Long called Dungeon Mill, this is an early-seventeenth-century fulling mill. FCR 1834 shows J & T C Wrigley in this mill. It was later taken over by Thornton, Marsden & Vickerman. The name was changed in the 1950s. Now industrial units, with some mending being done.
Phoenix Mill	In 1857 it was used by Joseph Schofield, cotton spinners; in 1950 Haigh & Oakes, woollen manufacturers, were operating here.
Rashcliffe Mill	FCR 1834 refers to this mill, rebuilt by Tom Nelson & Co. In the 1870s Blamires & Co were here, but *c.* 1890 Messrs Taylor & Lodge moved in and are still here today.
Scarr Mill	Nathaniel Berry was in this mill in the later nineteenth century. In 1910 it was in use by E H Sellars & Co.
Victoria Mill	This was built in the 1840s by J W & H Shaw; the firm of E & A Priest also leased rooms. In 1910 it was used by William Shaw (Victoria Mill) Ltd.

Meltham township

Albion Mill	By the beginning of the twentieth century this housed Allen Taylor & Co and J R Maudsley & Co. It is now occupied by R Butterworth, a textiles firm.
Bent Ley Mill	Part of the Brook family story, this mill was built *c.* 1840, with warehouse, offices and dyehouse being added later. There was further expansion in 1890. Bent Ley Silk Mill Ltd worked this mill, later changing to cotton thread.
Brigg Mill	J B Bentley was in this mill in 1891; J Walker & Co were here in 1910; it is now Sunbank Textiles.
Brow Mills	There is a reference to Brow Mills in YTD in 1910, when it housed Sam Beaumont, yarns.
Lower Sunny Bank Mill	Joseph Taylor of Golcar (see Victoria Mills) leased this mill in 1847 and remained until their move to Spink Mire Mill in 1854. J W Denham leased the mill for a time but it was sold off in 1905.
Meltham Mill	A Dartmouth estate scribbling and fulling mill from the eighteenth century, it was first used as a cotton factory by William Brook. Jonas Brook made it one of the largest cotton factories in Yorkshire. FCR 1834 suggests both cotton and silk

were produced; the firm entered cotton yarn in the 1851 Great Exhibition. They continued to expand the buildings, adding further mills, gasworks and a dyehouse. In 1931 it was taken over by United Thread Co and closed down. The Brook family were extensively involved in developing the area – funding the building of workers' housing, schools, churches, convalescent home, the Carlile Institute and Meltham Town Hall. Their name crops up on many of the committees formed to run Huddersfield Corporation and its outlying townships.

Mill Moor mill   See Sefton Mill.

New Bridge Mill   The firm of Ramsden & Halstead were here in the mid-1850s and may have been the forerunner of Messrs Walker & Ramsden, who in 1863 suffered a fire.[29] In 1910 it was occupied by William Pearson & Co.

Royd Edge Mill   Ramsden, Mellor & Co leased this mill *c.*1840; it is shown as a woollen mill in 1854. About 30 years later, Jonas Brook & Co expanded onto this site, also known as Royd Edge Dyeworks.

Scarbottom Mill   This was built by the Meltham Spinning Company *c.*1886 as a steam-powered, five-storey mill; demolished 1989.

Sefton Mill   FCR 1834 shows this mill as built in 1818. John Eastwood & Sons were the owners. William Halstead & Sons were at this address for the first half of the twentieth century.

Shoe Broads Mill   See Sefton Mill.

Spink Mire Mill   This was an old fulling mill used by James Rawcliffe in the 1830s. Ainley & Taylor (see Victoria Mills, Golcar) were here for a time in the 1850s. Ainley left the firm and Joseph Taylor & Sons remained until their move to Victoria Mills. The firm

Spink Mire Mill.

of Quarmby & Sykes, shoddy & mungo, were here at the end of the nineteenth century and remained for over 50 years.

Upper Sunny   James Shaw were here in 1851; by 1910 the mill was occupied
Bank Mill   by A T Woodhead & Sons, yarn spinners.

Netherthong township
Alma Mill   Joseph Mellor & Sons used it from mid-1850s to *c.*1900.

Thongsbridge Mill   A fulling and carding mill, built in the 1770s (according to FCR 1834) when Joseph Robinson was in the mill, it was later taken over by George Mellor, which became J Mellor & Sons. It was advertised for sale or to let in 1882.[30] Thongsbridge Spinning Company and B Vickerman & Sons were here at start of twentieth century. Now units.

New Mill township
Kirkbridge Mill   In 1800 the New Mill Cotton Company were at this mill; in 1867 Henry Pontefract rented part of it. From 1890 Graham & Barnfather were here for a number of years, and then became Graham & Pott Ltd.

Valley Mills   Jonathan Thorpe & Sons occupied this mill for the first half of the twentieth century.

Scholes township
Lee Mill   Battye & Farrar, woollen manufacturers, leased part of this mill in the mid-1850s; YTD 1910 shows Lockwood Bros, shoddy & mungo. Thomas Birkhead & Sons, dyers, were here in 1950.

South Crosland township
Armitage Bridge Mill   John Brooke & Sons moved *c.*1819 to this integrated mill, housing all parts of the textile process. Originally it used both hand-power and water-power; steam was added when the six-storey mill was built *c.*1829. In 1838 a new weaving shed was added and further buildings as the business expanded. Workers' cottages were also built on the site. It is now units, some of which are textiles.

Queen's Square Mill   By 1848 Vickerman & Beaumont were operating from this mill, before Josiah France moved there *c.*1880. Josiah France eventually moved into Kirkheaton Mills (q.v.) as part of the Illingworth Morris Group.

Steps Mill   The earliest reference to this fulling and scribbling mill is 1707, when the Roberts family were here. The families of Beaumont & Vickerman seem to have gone in and out of partnership with each other in this mill over the next fifty

Armitage Bridge Mill.

years, but finally the Vickermans went to Taylor Hill Mill and control passed to Joshua Beaumont & Co.

Thongsbridge township
Pickwick Mill	Still occupied by Sam Weller & Co.
Royds Mill	This has been converted to housing.

Upperthong township
Albion Mill	Ben Mellor & Sons were in this mill from *c.*1840 until at least the First World War.
Bridge Mill (Riverholme Works)	James Brooke & Sons were here before moving to Bradley Mills in 1856. Fred Lawton had part of this mill in 1919.
Prickleden Mill (Upper Mill)	In the 1860s it was used by James Holmes & Sons. After that it was let to various firms. By 1906 it was disused.
Spring Lane Mill	Built *c.*1840, this mill is mentioned in a trade directory of 1857, which shows it used by William Lockwood. He ran it until *c.*1870 when Jonas Brook & Co took over.

Wooldale township
Choppard's Mill	Built *c.*1815, this mill was used by Tom Moorhouse & Co in the 1840s and Eli Wimpenny in the 1860s.
Cuttell Mill	FCR 1834 shows J Cuttell & Bros in the mill.
Ford Mill	Messrs Wood & Burtt, yarn spinners, occupied this mill in

1910. It was later taken over by Paton & Baldwins, who made knitting wools.

Glendale Mill   This scribbling and fulling mill was built about the 1780s by J Kenworthy. By 1900 Messrs Bower, Roebuck & Firth were using this mill, the partnership changing to Bower & Roebuck in 1910. This firm is still in the mill.

Holmfirth Mills   FCR 1834 has J & G Gartside and Charlesworth & Sons both using this mill. N Thewlis & Co were in the mill in 1852 when the Bilberry Reservoir burst its bank, causing great loss of life and damage, which included this mill.

Ing Nook Mill   A small early mill.

Midge Mill   Shown just outside Thick Hollins on an 1854 map. Also known as Scholes Mill.

New Mill   New Mill Cotton Spinning Co.

Scholes Mill   See Midge Mill.

Shaley Wood Bottom Mill   See Ford Mill.

Stoney Bank Mill   Built as a woollen mill in the early nineteenth century, it was one of the mills involved in the 1842 Plug Riots, when strikers removed plugs on boilers to prevent others going to work. The new mill, built *c.*1850 of five storeys, used both water and steam power. Charles Moon was at this mill until his death, when Denton Brothers took over and operated as Charles Moon (Successors) Ltd. In the mid-1970s it was converted to industrial units for various purposes. The main buildings have been demolished.

Underbank Mill   Probably an early fulling and scribbling mill, this was converted to woollens by the mid-nineteenth century. Occupied by Roebuck & Sandford by 1910, a firm that later became William Sandford & Son.

Wildspur Mill   Built in the mid-nineteenth century, this mill was operated by Edward Hirst & Sons for many years. Copley, Marshall & Co, textile manufacturers, had moved in by 1910 and still operated from the mill in 1950.

Chapter Six
Colne Valley

View over the Colne valley.

An area closely associated with textile mills, the Colne valley has steep sides, many tributary streams and rough grazing for sheep. Originally an area of scattered hamlets over the higher land, the hillsides were used for producing the wool, drying the washed yarn and drying the cloth, spread out on tenterhooks.

The early small mills were built up here before improvements in transport and the use of steam power encouraged the development of housing and mills on the valley bottom alongside the canal, the railway

Yarn drying out on the hillside.

Weavers' cottages which are now Colne Valley Museum.

and the road to Manchester. Its proximity to Lancashire is probably the reason that many of the early textile mills were cotton. There are still many characteristic weavers' cottages dotting the hillsides. Three such cottages house the Colne Valley Museum, which shows how the industry developed from its smallest beginnings.

Ramsden Mill

The Ramsdens owned much of the land around Huddersfield, but it is not certain how those who owned the mill in Golcar were related to the more prominent family.

Ramsden Mill is one of the older mills built near the river to utilise its power. In 1672 Hugh Ramsden, of Hilltop in Quarmby, granted the lease of the fulling mill and lands to Edmund Walker, salter, and William Bradley, salter.[1] Yet, just a few years

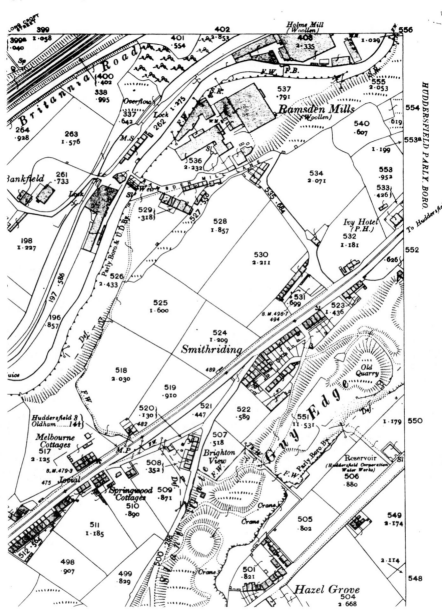

Ordnance Survey map 1893: scale 25″ to 1 mile.

later, Hugh granted a half share in the fulling mill at Golcar to George Dawson of
Dodlee in Longwood 'for and in consideration of the sum of five shillings of lawfull
money of Englande to him in hand paid by the said George Dawson'.

Many mills changed names to reflect the owners or occupiers, and this document shows that the early name for Ramsden Mill was Sykrehouse, where it refers to a

> half part of all that messuage ... fulling mill having in it two wheels commonly called or known by the name of Sykrehouse Mill
>
> January 1678[2]

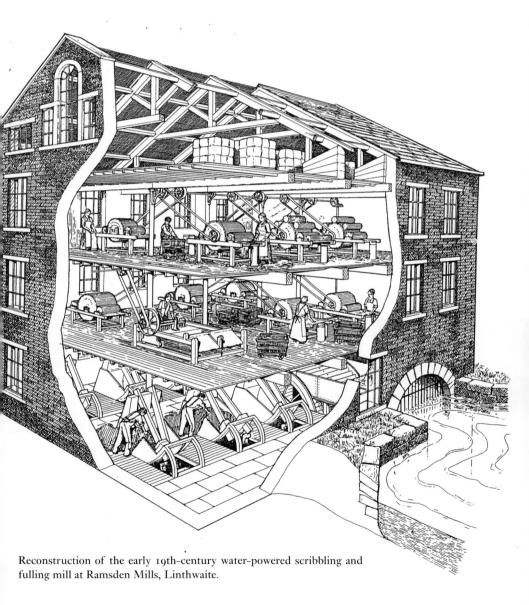

Reconstruction of the early 19th-century water-powered scribbling and fulling mill at Ramsden Mills, Linthwaite.

Later, a mill was built in the township of Linthwaite and known as New Mill. As successive generations held the mills, ownership was split among a number of children. When a later Hugh Ramsden died in 1789, the mills were left in eight-part ownership among his five sons, Hugh, Lawrence, Robert, James and Richard, his two daughters – Mary, wife of Joshua Hall, and Elizabeth, wife of John Varley of Shaw Carr Wood Mills – and his grandson, John Batley.[3]

Ten years later, the mills were leased, with both Upper and Lower mills advertised and described as having 'four drivers and six fallers all in good condition, driven by 2 water wheels'.

A further deed of 1826[4] names Hugh Ramsden of Ramsden Mill in Golcar, James Ramden of Ramsden Mill, John son of James Ramsden, Robert Ramsden, John Batley, William Hall, Eli Walker and Mary his wife, Elizabeth Walker, Sarah Hall, Joshua Woodhouse, Elizabeth Varley, John Ramsden of Slaithwaite, James Ramsden of Wellhouse and John White and Anne his wife and John Varley. The continual splitting-up of ownership in this way was to lead to endless arguments and eventually litigation.

This old mill building was built over the River Colne, with a wheel arch under the mill to provide water power, and was originally used for scribbling and fulling.

It had fulling stocks on the ground floor, powered by the water-wheel, carding engines on the first floor, carding and scribbling engines on the second floor, and storage for the bales of wool in the attic. Though the mill itself is now in poor condition, the blocked-up outline of the wheel arch can still be seen.

The twin functions of scribbling – cleaning and carding (combing) the raw wool onto cops ready for spinning – and fulling – pounding woollen cloth in large troughs

Water-wheel archway, now blocked up.

Ramsden Mill, 1981.

of warm water and soap to give a felted cloth which can then be finished in various ways – were often 'public'. The individual weaver took his raw wool to the mill to be scribbled, returned home to spin and weave it and then returned the piece of cloth to the mill, where the miller fulled it along with other pieces of cloth from various other weavers in the area.

Fulling was one of the earliest processes to be mechanised and was often the prerogative of the Lord of the Manor, who obtained a useful income from the process.

The Ramsden mills were expanded to a large four-storey building with central tower, standing near the original mill. A large chimney towered over the site, with a brick-built channel to funnel the fumes from the steam engine. The chimney is still there, but only a gaping hole in the hillside shows where the channel once ran.

A horrific accident occurred in the mill in 1853[5] when a man by the name of Spencer was putting a strap on a drum in the mill. The strap caught hold of his smock and 'whirled him round the drum'. The accident was not noticed until 'his heels were heard knocking against the ceiling' by which time his head had been torn off and 'his bowels scattered about on the floor'.

Ramsden Mill Company

On 17 July 1864,[6] the Ramsden family transferred their interests in the property to the Ramsden Mill Co. The parties were listed as Thomas Ramsden, his wife Ann; William Ramsden and Nancy Ramsden, widow; Thomas Cliffe of Paddock; Peggy Varley of Linthwaite, widow; William Varley of Lingards, brewer; James Varley of Netherton, stone merchant; John Varley of Notthingham, surgeon; Betty Varley, Linthwaite, spinster; Humphery and Ann Sykes of Manchester; and Allici Ramsden of Ramsden Mill, spinster. Many were descendants of the original owners.

The property consisted of cottages and other buildings then occupied by the Ramsden Mill Co at what was known as New Mill in Linthwaite, the fulling mill in the township of Golcar called the Old Mill, the cottage buildings nearby commonly called the Mill House, and the fulling mill and scribbling mills in Linthwaite formerly called the New Mill, together with the woods and ground in Linthwaite called the West Wood, the Holme wyne and the Headland wood.

However, there remained controversy over ownership of the shares, resulting in a battle in the High Court of Chancery. The court eventually decided that the mill should be sold in two lots. This sale took place in 1875 when Lot 1, the old mill, was put up for sale at auction, the bidding starting at £5,000. It was finally sold to John Edward Ramsden for £12,050. He also bought Lot 2, the rest of the property, for the sum of £3,000 and 'thus the present occupants will now become the owner of all the property'.[7]

Sketch of Ramsden Mill complex, 1877.

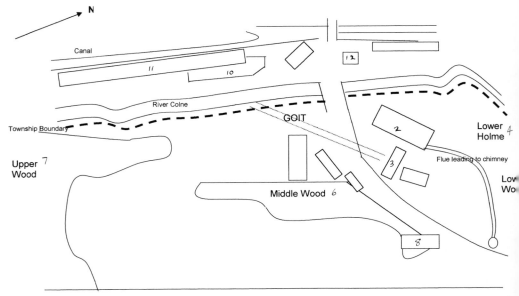

By 1876 the firm was known as Messrs Thomas Ramsden & Son. That year yet another fire began in the drying store of the mill. Garsham Tiffany, the engine tenter (engineer who looked after the engines and boilers which provided power to the mill), spotted the fire about 9 in the morning and sounded the whistle. All the workers around the mill ran with cans and buckets to throw water on the burning material in the store.

The material consisted of 1,000lb of waste so would have been highly inflammable. The fire brigade from Messrs Joseph Taylor & Sons at Victoria Mills arrived very quickly and within half an hour of its starting, the fire was extinguished with only £100 worth of damage done. By the time other brigades arrived, they were not needed.

The engineer's job was very important: without power, the whole mill would stop. The Tiffany family had only recently moved from Elland, presumably for better pay. Not only was Garsham employed in the mill, but his two eldest sons, Joe Edward and John William, found work there too.

A deed of 1877[8] gives both a list and a plan of the mill area. As the property lay across the township boundary, it was listed separately, though not all the given numbers appeared on the deed extract:

Property In Linthwaite

No	Property
1	Piece of waste land at corner of weir
2	Middle Holme being site of new mill and works
3	Site of old mill gasworks and stove
4	Lower Holme grass meadow
5	Lower wood
6	Middle wood
7	Upper wood
8	Site of cottages and offices
9	And a small plot of land called little wood on opposite side severed from above by the turnpike road

Property In Golcar

10	Fulling and scribbling mill and land
11	Reservoir
12	Dyehouse and old cottage

Whether the firm was in financial difficulties or just did not require so much space is unknown, but in 1880 the New Mill was sold to David and Arthur Whitwam.[9]

A fire in the old mill in 1894, caused by friction in a condenser on the fourth floor of the mill, spread rapidly. As soon as the workers saw the fire, they got to work with buckets to try to control the flames and prevent it spreading to the floors below. As there was a danger that the fire could spread to the premises of Whitwam & Co nearby, the Huddersfield Corporation fire brigade was sent for.

Ramsden Mill.

When they arrived, they considered that there was an 'awkward road to the mill which is in a hollow with the canal on one side and the river on the other', so the crew waited with their engine on Manchester Road to see if they were really needed. Fortunately they weren't and things were soon under control, though over £4,000 of damage was done.

The track down to the mill caused many problems for the firm. Goods had to be transported on ponies up the track to Manchester Road, further up the valley side, before the goods could be transferred to wagons for transport to customers.

By 1899 the firm of William Whiteley was using the mill and at this time was charged with employing a person under the age of 16 without a medical certificate confirming that he was fit to be employed.

Despite pleading that this was merely an oversight and the boy, Falmage Thorpe (who was 15), was perfectly healthy, the firm was fined 10s. (50p) plus 13s. (65p) costs. The boy's father should have known better since he was a boot and shoe manufacturer, employing others himself. The Thorpes were a local family, all born and bred in Golcar.

Taylor & Livesey Ltd

The firm of Taylor & Livesey, owned by Charlie Kaye Taylor and Arthur Livesey, moved into Ramsden Mills about 1898, when they transferred their knitwear plant from mills in Paddock.[10] They traded successfully there for many years, eventually buying the mills in 1920 from Whitwam & Co.[11]

The two world wars meant changes at Ramsden Mills, as at other mills. Workers tended to be the older men and women, or sometimes unskilled workers from elsewhere. This tradition continued, with bus loads of women arriving from Barnsley and other south Yorkshire towns to help fill the vacancies in the mills.

The Korean war affected the supply of raw materials, making continued production difficult. The recessions and competition of the twentieth century eventually caused losses and by 1974 the firm were beginning to make redundancies.

Modernisation is no proof against fire and so it proved at this mill in 1979[12] when a couple of youngsters decided to make a den just outside the mill building, lighting candles and causing a fire that gutted the weaving and knitting sheds, with a loss of the jersey-knitting machinery and £250,000 worth of damage.

However, one of the reasons for Huddersfield's general success in textiles is a willingness to diversify into other branches of the trade. Taylor & Livesey began to produce furniture fabrics, being invited in 1983 to take part in the International Wool Secretariat collection promotion show in Birmingham.[13]

Whilst this kept the firm going for some time, within five years Ramsden Mills were closed, with the loss of 75 jobs. The contents were sold over a two-day auction and the mills finally shut in July 1988.[14]

Taylor & Livesey had been at the mill for 90 years, and in its heyday had employed over 250 workers. They had also been in production in Shaw Carr Wood Mills, Paddock Mills, Albion Mills and Gledholt Mills.

Ramsden Mill – owner's house.

Modern Times

However, this wasn't to be the end of the story. Whilst the mills are no longer used by the textile trade, the firm of Trojan Plastics Ltd bought the site and it has begun a new lease of life as a production centre for acrylic baths and shower trays.

The 'new' four-storey mill eventually became unsafe and was demolished, but the old mill still clings to existence, though in a very poor state. New, more appropriate buildings for modern production are filling the site, but the mill owner's house has found a new use as offices.

Shaw Carr Wood Mill

The upper part of the Colne Valley reaches up to the border with Lancashire around Saddleworth. An early turnpike road, built by John Metcalfe (Blind Jack of Knaresborough) leads across the moorland and the old mileposts can still be seen marking the way across desolate moorland.

Ordnance Survey map 1893: scale 25″ to 1 mile.

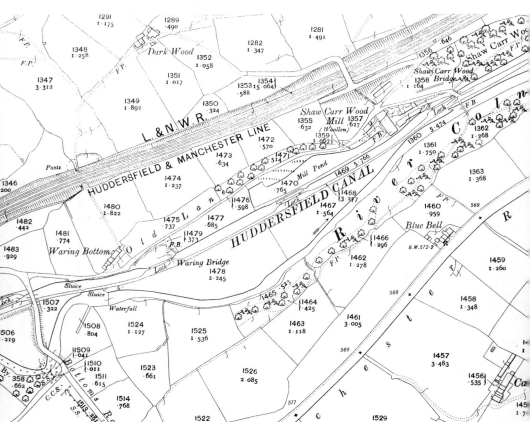

Whilst the woollen industry in the West Riding was still largely a cottage industry, cotton production in Lancashire was being mechanised. This process gradually spread over the Pennines along these old routes, giving rise to a Yorkshire cotton industry, which has long been overshadowed by the immense growth in the production of woollen and worsted.

Baines' 1822 Trade Directory describes Slaithwaite as having 'several large cotton mills and woollen factories in which a great many work people are employed'. Some cotton was still being produced in this area into the twentieth century, supplying the local mills which mixed wool with other fibres, including cotton, in their fabrics.

But capital is needed in order to build factories. Whilst some clothiers could start by expanding on an existing loom shop or small workshop, many mills were built from scratch.

About the beginning of the nineteenth century there was a boom in speculative building, some of which was financed by landowners looking for a good return on their money. In August 1785 John Varley wrote to Lord Dartmouth, the principal landowner in Slaithwaite, stating that:

> The improvement of the manufactory in our neighbourhood increasing so much inclines me to build a new scribbling mill which I can with convenience a little above my corn mill if your lordship approve of it, but as the expense will be considerable and having laid out so much in improving the corn mill and the housing, should be much obliged if your lordship will advance me £100 at interest for which I will pay £5 per cent half yearly …
>
> PS I have got an estimate of the expense which without engines will amount to more than £200 – your lordship's sentiments on this subject to Mr Elmsall or myself will oblige.

The Varleys were an extensive family, responsible for building and expanding many of the mills in the valley, including the Corn Mill in Slaithwaite itself. They gave their name to Varley Road, which runs out of Slaithwaite towards Meltham. John's son, Richard, went on to become Dartmouth's agent in the area, as well as managing and part-owning Waterside Mill, another cotton mill.

Richard's brother John ran the Corn Mill and was also in partnership with another brother at Shaw Carr Wood Mills. These were built about 1787, when John Varley senior was given a lease of 42 years at £20 per annum. The mill was close to the canal and River Colne, giving it modern transport and a good source of water power.

The Dartmouth terrier describes a three-storey mill of 26yd by 12yd (24 × 11m) and a two-storey mill of 12yd by 6yd (11 × 5.5m). There was also a 10hp steam engine; though rather small, it could be used to supplement water power in times of drought. By 1828 a new engine of 20hp was needed.

The water for the dam was drawn from the river, passed underneath the canal and was then fed back into the river by way of another covered goit.

Although parts of the mill were let out to other clothiers in the area, it was mainly run by Messrs Dyson & Varley, though their partnership is not shown in the Trade

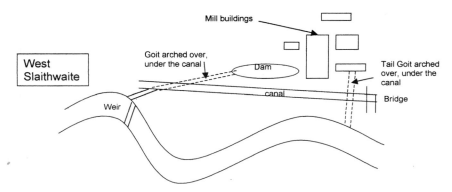

Sketch plan of Shaw Carr Wood Mill 1790s, Dartmouth Estate papers.

Directory of 1822. That mentions only Thomas Varley, scribbling miller of Lingards, and John Varley, corn miller of Lingards.

However, a 21-year lease of 1806 was taken by John and Joseph Varley together with John Dyson. This lease included a clause that the buildings must be insured for £700 and that the banks of the mill dam and river nearby should be kept repaired. This partnership remained in the mill, certainly for the next twenty years or so.

Factory Commission Inquiry

The 1834 report to the Factory Commissioners[15] shows that the firm of Dyson & Varley employed 85 people – 23 men and 62 women – who were paid on a 'time' basis. In almost all cases the women were earning less than the men, but there is nothing to indicate what jobs they were doing. The oldest men, aged 21 and over, were earning 16s. 9d. (84p) a week, whilst the same age group for women were only earning 6s. 2d. (31p).

The youngest children, 10 to 12 years of age, were earning 2s. 6d. (boys) or 2s. (girls). They would be employed cleaning under the machines, or as 'pieceners' who had to join together the broken threads to keep the looms running.

Many of the children worked alongside, or for, their parents, who were responsible for paying them their wages. The owners specifically state that, although they do not need to employ young children, they take them on 'chiefly to satisfy the parents who have older children here'. Presumably the parents had nowhere else to leave the children and needed the wages.

In common with most other mills, the day started at 6 am and continued until about 7.30 pm, with only a half-hour break at 8 am and an hour at noon. In this mill, the owners said the machinery was all stopped whilst the workers took their breaks, though this was not always the case, either here or elsewhere.

Holidays were unpaid and consisted of:

Three whole days at Christmas, two days at Easter, two at Whitsuntide, or sometimes only 2 half days for these last two and two whole days at the feast time in August.

Unlike many other mill owners, this firm kept records of how many hours the mill had worked per quarter during the year 1832. These were:

	1st quarter	2nd quarter	3rd quarter	4th quarter
Days worked	78	76	76	77
Hours worked	912¾	874	862¼	855¼

It is easy to see from this that an average day was about 11 hours in length. This masks the fact that some days would have been shorter because of loss of water-power during droughts and some days would have been much longer if trade was brisk.

When questioned about keeping the mills working at night by employing a second shift of workers, they were adamant that they did not do this and considered it unnecessary and harmful:

> We would particularly advise the moving power be stopped in all mills and factories (except corn mills) during the night from nine pm – six am. As to the hours of labour we believe that eleven or eleven and a half exclusive of meal times and nine hours on Saturday would be better for the health of the work people but if the time is shortened beyond that the wages will be generally reduced; besides this, it will have a tendency to drive the English manufacturer, in a great measure, to other nations.

The commission was also concerned about the plight of the worker when accidents happened. Dyson & Varley admitted that they did not give any sick pay, but always paid for a surgeon in the event of accidents in the mill – though they were quick to point out that they hadn't had to do so recently and 'then only for slight ones'. They were most indignant at the thought that, as managers of the mill, they should be held liable for any accidents:

> We consider and so do most people we have conversed with on the subject that it would be very arbitrary to make the masters, or we may say the employers of the poor, liable to be indicted and sent to a prison for manslaughter; in some case of accidents which it is not possible always to prevent; it would in some cases stop the concern and throw people out of work and out of bread because it would take the active master away and the workpeople belonging to it.

Regarding the child workers, Dyson & Varley explained that if children came up to a quarter of an hour late they would be fined one penny and if half an hour late, a quarter of a day's pay was taken off. Those by the piece were not fined, though it was not stated if the workers were let in at any time during the day or if they had to arrive at a set time, as in many other factories.

Corporal punishment was specifically barred, according to the owners' statement, and the overlookers were told to send home any children who would not behave and not touch them in any way.

Final Days

In the 1870s Henry Walker had moved into the mill and soon managed to set fire to it. Fortunately, the fire was spotted and quickly extinguished.[16]

When Henry Walker died in 1905, he was described as a Baptist and Tory. He had worked from Britannia Mills, Crosland Moor, as well as Shaw Carr Wood Mills. He had also built the Commercial Mills in Slaithwaite in 1876, but these had not been as successful as his venture at Shaw Carr Wood.

William Hirst of Marsden, at the head of the Colne Valley, then took a 21-year lease on Shaw Carr Wood Mill in 1881 at £150 p.a. rental from the Earl of Dartmouth, but by 1910 it was part of Joseph Beaumont junior's works making worsted, serges and art furnishing cloths. The firm also used Colne Mills and by the First World War had moved their production out of Shaw Carr Wood Mills.[17]

Taylor & Livesey Ltd continued production in Shaw Carr Wood for a number of years and bought the mills in 1917 from the Dartmouth estate.[18] The area was then described as having a small pond and tenter field, a mill pond, mill, boiler-house, store, teasing place, office, warehouse, stable, cottage, garden and land around the mill pond.

There was never a huge amount of production undertaken there and eventually, just before the Second World War, the mill buildings were sold off and demolished for the stone, which was reused elsewhere. The remains of the goits can still be seen from the canalside walk.

Victoria Mills

Ainley & Taylor

In 1805 Joseph Taylor was born in Golcar, to a relatively poor family. At the age of 7,[19] he began work in Ramsden Mill as one of the 'piecers'. These children had to twist together the strands of yarn as they were being woven.

Whilst the work may not have been arduous in one sense, the yarn cut into the young flesh and their fingers would often be sore and bleeding. But woe betide any youngster who allowed blood to get onto the yarn, as this could stain the piece and reduce its value. The hours were long, getting up at dawn to reach the mill on time and returning home in the dark. His father often had to carry the lad to work at first.

Young Joseph became a weaver, but also learned the trade of a slubber, as part of preparing the wool for spinning. He went on to work for Starkey Brothers in Longroyd Bridge and then in one of the mills in Lockwood.

But Joseph had grander ideas and was prepared to work for them. He saved all the bits of waste from his weaving jobs until he had sufficient to weave a piece of cloth for himself. He took his single piece of cloth and sold it for the grand sum of one guinea (£1.05).

Unfortunately, he was paid this amount in a bank note. At that time banks were small, family-run firms and often failed, going 'bankrupt', and this is what happened in Joseph's case. As there was no insurance or compensation in those days, he lost all his capital. Despite this setback, he continued saving and working up his little bits of waste material until he was able to build up a small business of his own.

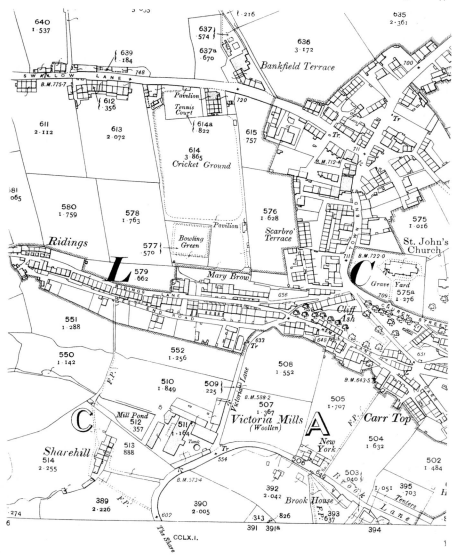

Ordnance Survey map 1907: scale 25″ to 1 mile.

In his forties, he went into partnership with John Ainley as scribbling millers, taking a lease on Sunny Bank Mill in Meltham. Just before that lease was due to end, they bought Spink Mire Mill, improved and rebuilt it, and moved in all their old machinery.

In the same year as this move, 1853, the two men went into partnership with John and Samuel Walker to build another mill in Golcar. This mill may have also been

Date plaque.

known as Golcar Mills, though the reference is unclear, but the name Victoria Mills was certainly given when it was completed in 1854.

Taylor & Ainley then traded as partners in a manufacturing enterprise that lasted for almost ten years. It was dissolved in 1863, though it was a further four years before the Taylor family were able to buy out the Ainley share of the business. Sam Walker's share of the business was sold to John Pearson, another Golcar clothier.

Victoria Mill, with oldest buildings in foreground.

Messrs Taylor & Walker were certainly there during the 1870s, as there is a record of the buildings being used by the Methodists for one of their annual camps, when 'a vast number of people assembled' to hear speeches and take part in a 'love feast'.[20]

The firm also decided to have separate, purpose-built offices. These were built, together with a cottage, looking towards Share Hill. They have now been demolished but can be seen in the aerial view.

The plans, drawn up by John Kirk and Sons in 1886, show what appears to be an ornate corner entrance, with counter facing and desks around the sides of the office. The cottages differ slightly from the original design, which may indicate a later extension or a change in plans.

Albion Mills in Golcar was also bought by Taylor & Sons and in total the firm employed over 250 people in the Colne Valley.

The firm not only established the usual mill fire brigade but also provided uniforms and fire engine. They took an active interest in ensuring that the equipment was used efficiently, and this was put to the test one morning in 1862, when the fire bell rang at the mill and all the people in the area rushed out of their houses to help put out the fire and also to see the new fire engine swung into action. Fortunately, the fire proved to be in the teazing room, in an outhouse. There was a great deal of smoke, but little damage was done.

The family were staunch Methodists, with a definite work-and-service ethic. In 1836, Joseph joined a small band of New Connection Methodists who met in a small cottage. Eventually they were able to build the Wellhouse Chapel and later the Providence Chapel at Golcar Hill. The Taylor family provided a great deal of the funds for these. Joseph gave 1s. 6d. (7½p) to everyone over 60 in Golcar each Christmas.

He was also a far-sighted and generous man. He was a member of the Local Board of Guardians and tried to persuade them to provide clean water for the local people. The board refused to do this, so Joseph set to and built two reservoirs of his own, laying pipes to almost 300 houses in Golcar. He was also involved in providing gasworks for the village.

Having received his own early education at the old Town School, he went on to teach there, became a trustee and was instrumental in ensuring its transition to a new Board School. His son, Charles Henry, carried on this tradition, serving at the school and on the local board.

Joseph also required his workforce to obey the rules he had drawn up for his mills. In 1863 he took Sam Shaw, a slubber, to court for neglect of his work. Joseph's rules stated that 14 days' notice must be given to terminate employment. Sam had been given notice but chose to leave the next day instead of working the fortnight. Joseph claimed 30s. (£1.50) expenses and compensation for having to get someone else to finish the work. The man eventually agreed to go back to work out his notice, but whether Joseph ever got the compensation he claimed is not recorded.

This was not the only time the family found itself in court. Joseph's son was sued for damages when he seduced the daughter of the local publican. Although he agreed to marry her, and the wedding was arranged, he failed to turn up and the girl's father successfully claimed damages. The child resulting from the liaison went on to form the successful firm of Crabtree & Co, which was in Ramsden Mill for a time.

Pearson Brothers

Alongside Taylor & Sons, the business of Pearson Brothers also worked in Victoria Mill. John Pearson's four sons, Ramsden, Albert, Joseph Dyson and Henry Edward, converted the business to a limited company in 1896 when each took one share. One share also went to each of their wives.

The firm continued to expand, extending the buildings in 1905. Just before the First World War, over 9,000 spindles were operating in this mill with 82 looms. The firm also owned Commercial Mills in Slaithwaite, which they bought from Henry Walker, where a further 44 looms were kept fully employed.

The next generation of Pearsons – Ernest and Harold (Ramsden's sons); Frank and John Edward (Albert's sons); and Donald Rupert and Joseph Sykes (Henry Edward's sons) – also went into the business. Joseph Sykes Pearson was tragically killed on the western front in November 1918, just before the signing of the Armistice and is buried in Calais.

An insurance plan of 1955 shows how extensive the buildings had become and the aerial view allows us to see how the mill developed from the small buildings in the centre, with the main building towering over them. Further sheds were added, but

Victoria Mill, Golcar.

the cottages at the bottom left were demolished in the 1980s to allow for further expansion.

Whilst reclaimed wool was used for part of the yarn, virgin wool made up the bulk of the supply, arriving in the mill in its raw state, often from local farms. On arrival, the wool would be sorted into its different grades and then scoured to remove the grease, though the lanolin produced in the process was stored in huge barrels and sold on to other businesses.

After this the wool could be washed and spun onto coppins, from which the bobbin-winders then filled the bobbins for weaving. Bobbin-winding was a relatively popular job – not too dirty. 'We used to sing to pass the time even though the bosses didn't like it. They kept telling us to get on with the job, which we did, but we sang as well,' some former employees told me.

The weavers had to make do with whatever yarn they were given, but were still expected to produce good cloth. They were paid by the piece or cut, and at first would not be paid unless a complete cut of 70 yards (64m) was finished. 'One young man had just got married, and he had so many problems with poor yarn and flying shuttles that he didn't finish any length of cloth and so started his married life on a week's wage of nothing.'

After weaving, the fabric went for its first mending, then was scoured and washed. Next came burling (picking out the tiny bits of loose yarn), perching (looking for and marking any areas that needed mending), knotting (looking for, unpicking and sewing in any knots tied or twisted into the yarn when weaving), and then finish-mending

Loom beam ready for use.

Mending and finishing about 1900.

when the cloth was checked over again. After this it would be pressed, measured and packed as required.

Mending is quite a skilled job. To learn it, the youngster had to find someone who was prepared to take them on. 'Not only didn't we get paid, but our parents had to pay the person who was training us!' After this, if they could find a job, they could expect to earn a small wage, out of which they paid the mender who oversaw their job for at least another 6 months. Some of the Good Companion ladies said:

> In the 1930s wages were about 19s. [95p] a week for a 48 hour week, starting at 7 in the morning and not finishing before 5 at night.

Once skilled they would be paid by the piece of 70yd (64m). It was backbreaking work: the cloth was folded on the floor and run up over a bar, down onto an angled board or table where the mender had to check to find broken threads and sew them back in. Once the girls became really skilled, they could become finish menders, who checked the cloth once again after all the various processes to ensure there were no damaged sections of the cloth.

Although the workers got on well together, there was always some friction. The menders considered themselves a bit above the weavers, because their job was relatively clean, whereas the weavers' job was dirty. The weavers retaliated by referring to 'maungy menders'. But most agreed that their job was 'dirty, smelly and we got paid a pittance for doing it'.

The buildings had been expanded to include weaving sheds and other work space, and in 1965 the firm won a total of eight gold medals at the Trade Fair in Sacramento, California – more than any other British firm at the fair. Even so, in the end worsening trade conditions caused Pearson Brothers to transfer their work to their mill in Guiseley and in 1972 the mill closed.[21]

F Drake & Son

In 1887,[22] the firm of F Drake & Son was started in a room in Victoria Mills rented by Joshua Drake. He named the company 'F Drake' hoping that his son Frank would take over, which eventually he did, along with his brother Henry and Uncle Fred.

In 1908 they required larger premises and so moved to Manor Mills, Golcar, built in 1887, where they continued to trade as 'garnetters' for many years. Within a few years, there followed a series of deaths in the family.

Drake family group: Back row: Amelia, Emily, Joshua, Melinda, Sarah Jane. Front row: John William, John, Jane, Fred.

Fred Drake (1864–1926).

In 1913 Joshua died aged 66, and the next year Frank died of pneumonia at only 30 years of age. In 1918, Fred's son Harry died of war wounds, but fortunately his other son, Percy, entered the firm. They worked together for only a few years, until Fred died of pneumonia in 1926.

Despite this, the firm survived and continued to thrive through the depression of the twenties and thirties, often using a horse and cart to collect the waste material or deliver to their customers. They continued to use this method of transport for many years, although later it became more of an advertising ploy.

The advent of synthetic materials caused some problems because the old machines were unable to cope with fibres such as nylon. The material came through the

Driving a four-in-hand for Drakes.

sorting bays, then being fed into the various machines which pulled or sliced the fibres apart and could be quite vicious.

The rag mill would often need to have the fibres pressed down and workers would climb inside the machine to 'tread' the fibres down again, just like treading grapes! But man-made fibres did not respond well to this sort of treatment and the firm struggled to maintain its profits.

Ultimately it was sold, but was soon bought back by Percy's daughter and his son-in-law, James Haigh, a textile designer and lecturer at what was then Huddersfield Polytechnic, now the University of Huddersfield. In 1965 they took over the business and succeeded in revitalising it, bringing in new machinery and new technology.

A 'Giant modern rag tearing machine made in Italy' was bought, which could do the work formerly done by nine separate machines, producing 60kg of rags per hour. 'Rags [are] simply fed into the machine and emerge as reprocessed fibre – all neatly packed and baled.'[23]

Continued expansion caused the firm to look for further premises and in 1972 they took over Victoria Mills, undertaking considerable improvement and renovations to take the new machinery. A subsidiary company called F Drake (Fibres) Ltd was formed to produce polypropylene fibres.

Despite a first-year slump, continued efficiency kept the business afloat and within a short time all debts were repaid and exports were up to 50% of production. They became the largest manufacturer of polypropylene in Europe. Further expansion soon followed, providing another 60 jobs.[24]

Three years later, the local paper was able to talk about a 'technological revolution in Colne Valley',[25] an area which has traditionally depended heavily on wool textiles. Although the firm was still engaged in the textile industry, both the fibres used and the markets in which they were sold had changed. By this time Drakes were producing fibres for the carpet, floor tile and upholstery industry in a highly automated plant, kept running night and day.

Although the Managing Director had originally seen production of the fibres in Italy, where it was pioneered, but James Haigh was almost the only British textile manufacturer to see its potential. He brought the equipment and the process to England and made the firm the largest of its kind in Britain. The new fibre was produced from polypropylene crystals, a waste product of the oil industry. The fibre was marketed under the name of Gymline, with 50% production sold direct to overseas customers.

In 1976, Drakes set up an overseas branch to sell on their obsolete machinery. The firm worked on the principle of replacing one machine each year, to ensure that they were always at the cutting edge of the new technology.

The firm continued to expand its production, both at Victoria Mills and at Manor Mills, with an emphasis on new technology and electronics, but still found time to organise a works trip out to Tadcaster's Toulton Polo Park to watch the finals of the F Drake Jubilee Plate, with a lunch for 400 people. This was a treat for the work people and the family to celebrate the firm's growing success.[26]

The family interest in polo was also useful as a marketing tool. Foreign visitors were invited to look round the mill, then were treated to a visit to a polo match before going home. It proved very popular with their customers.[27]

Further expansion meant the demolition in 1979 of a disused six-storey building at Victoria Mills, which was replaced with a single-storey unit equipped with modern machinery, which enabled an increase in weekly output from 120 tons to 200 tons.[28]

The end of the seventies saw major problems in all aspects of the textile industry and the UK carpet industry was no exception. It was hit by the strong pound, high interest rates and people not spending. The Australians increased their import duty on carpets by 20% as a reaction against cheap American imports, which was exactly the same problem that the UK carpet industry had.

Drakes concentrated on production of melt-spun polypropylene fibre under the brand name Gymlene and were hoping to gain extra business as a result of a new method of colour patterning. In 1980,[29] they won an order for £500,000 worth of business in Europe.

They put some of this success down to the amount of investment in machinery, which had made Drakes' factory one of the 'most modern of its type in Europe'.

Victoria Mill in the twentieth century.

These machines were running on a seven-day production cycle in order to supply the orders from three firms – two in Germany, one in Belgium – which were taking 700 tons of Drakes' fibre.

The next twelve years saw continued expansion and success for the firm. In 1981 they won the Queen's Award for Export Achievement and an award for safety in the mill. In a survey of the 'most safety conscious firms' Drake's had lower accident rates than the national average for their particular industry.

Queen's Award for Exports, 1988.

In Celebration of the Queen's Award to Industry for Export Achievement 1988 to.

"F. Drake & Company of Golcar Ltd"
Manor Mills, Golcar, England.

Mr & Mrs. James Haigh
Invite All Colleagues to the Presentation Ceremony
On Wednesday October 19th 1988

ARUNDEL Barry	CUSHING Anthony	HOBSON Kevin	NEWTON Robert
ARUNDEL Denis	EASTWOOD Darren	JACKSON David	PEEL Jeremy
ATKINSON Michael	EASTWOOD Wayne	JARMAN Ian	QUINN Michael
BALDWIN Brian	FANCHAMPS Andrew	JONES Ian	SCOTT Simon
BARDEN Michael	FELL Jonathan	KAYE Roger	SIMPSON Bradley
BARKER Stephen	FRANCE Betty	KAYE Nigel	SIMPSON Rueben
BENNETT Gary	GARBETT Jack	KIMMINGS Michael	SMITH David
BINKS Ian	GLEDHILL Andrew	KINDER Andrew	SORENSEN Kenneth
BLACKWELL Richard	HAIGH Christine	LENEGHAN Michael	TAYLOR Brian
BOOTHROYD Ian	HAIGH James	LITTLEWOOD Silvana	TAYLOR Marcus
BOULDER Stephen	HAIGH Joshua	MADIGAN Eamon	THORNBER Beverley
BOYES Vaughan	HALL Timothy	McCABE Paul	WADSWORTH Howard
BRAHNEY Graeme	HALLIGAN John	MESSENGER Rita	WALKER Timothy
BRAY Wayne	HAMER Andrew	MIDGLEY Paul	WARNER Paul
BROGDEN Ian	HARRIS Sydney	MILLER Daniel	WHITEHEAD Robert
BUSHELL Anthony	HENDRICKS Berris	MORAN Martin	WIGNALL James
CHADWICK Andrew	HIRST Geoffrey	MORTON Joan	WILSON Philip
COCK Patricia	HIRST Michael	NEWBOULD Dale	WRIGLEY Peter
COX Nicholas			

They also installed new silos and a £100,000 fully-automated silo storage and raw material handling system. In 1984, they moved further into new technology when they began producing heavy industrial-use fibres, a new generation of high-strength filament yarns under the name Leolene.[30]

Their building at Spa Fields industrial estate was the first new mill to be built in the Colne Valley since the Second World War and covered 51,670 sq. ft (4,800 sq. m), with a second stage planned for 1990. It was expected that the new mill would increase export potential, and confidence was high when they again won the Queen's Award for Exports.[31] Later, James Haigh was awarded the MBE for his services to exports.

F Drake (Fibres) Ltd was taken over by Readicut plc, but such was the firm's success that both James Haigh and Drakes' existing managing director were asked to remain with the firm.

The firm developed a biodegradable version of its fibres to help the environment. A secret ingredient was added, which caused the material to degrade over a given time and the amount could be varied to give a fibre that would degrade over six months or two years, according to ground conditions.

Drakes were quick to point out that this was not some potentially dangerous chemical they were adding, but a natural product that everyone in the country would know 'if we were to say it'.[32] Surprisingly, this was not the huge success that had been expected.

The firm continued to be involved in the local area, supporting the Lockwood Band and the Scapegoat Hill Band, sponsoring a Polo Tournament for the F Drake Silver Jubilee Plate and the Drake Huddersfield Cricket League.

Drake Extrusions

It was a considerable to shock to all when it was announced that Victoria Mills was to close, with a loss of 50 jobs, and operations were to be switched to Bradford.[33] After a period of redundancies and cutbacks, the firm has been able to continue and is now more confident of its future, with the new name of F Drake Extrusions.

Like so many other textile firms, the company has had to adapt and now produces short staples, which are sold for such diverse purposes as making tea bags or adding to concrete to strengthen it. This latter use is an adaptation of the old idea of adding hair (human or horse) to concrete.

Other Mills in the Area

Golcar township

Albion Mill	Built *c*.1865, this mill was used by Joseph Taylor (of Victoria Mills, q.v.), and Taylor & Livesey Ltd *c*.1915.
Beaufort Mill	G Whiteley & Co were here in 1911, according to YTD.
Golcar Mill	See Victoria Mill, Golcar.
Heath House Mill	Messrs Ainley & Taylor (see Victoria Mill, Golcar) were here in 1867; T W Thorpe Ltd were manufacturing wool here

Lees Mill, Golcar.

	during the Second World War. Now it is divided into industrial units, some of which are in textiles.
Holme Mill	A later mill used by Robert Taylor & Co, shoddy & mungo, at the end of the nineteenth century. John Lockwood & Co bought this mill in 1903.
Lees Mill	FCR 1834 gives Michael Lees in this mill, hence the name. Later John Crowther took it over but, when his sons moved to Britannia Mills in 1874, it was taken by Messrs Shaw & Berry. By 1910 it was already divided into units with some textile use.
Low Westwood Mill	Built before 1800; occupied by John, Jonathan, Joseph and Eli Shaw, according to FCR 1834. Joseph Hoyle leased part of it in the 1890s; W E Cotton, shoddy and mungo, moved here c.1900 and in 1977 suffered a fire.[34] YTD 1910 shows Colne Valley Spinning Co here also.
Manor Mills	See Victoria Mills in main text above for F Drake & Son, who were in this mill for many years.
Peep o' Day Mill	See Stanley Mill.
Ramsden Mill	See main text above.
Scarr Bottom Mill	There were rooms to let here in the 1860s; Eli Fielding is associated with the mill in 1884. By 1895 it was in the hands of John Lockwood & Sons, who remained for over fifty years.

Low Westwood Upper Mill.

Stanley Mill	Built *c.*1870 by Eli Fielding and Ben Whitwam, who became Whitwam & Co, still here in the twentieth century.
Titanic Mill	So named because it was built in 1912, this was the home of Colne Valley Spinning Co. Disused and almost ruined for many years, it is now being renovated and converted into sports facilities, shops, restaurants and some flats.
Town End Mill	Robert Taylor & Co are listed as shoddy & mungo merchants in this mill in 1910.
Victoria Mill	See main text above.

Titanic Mill.

Spring Grove Mill.

Linthwaite township

Black Rock Mill — Built *c.*1870s. Charles Lockwood & Sons moved here *c.*1880s. Florence E Lockwood, wife of Josiah, wrote *An Ordinary Life* about her experiences as a clothier's wife.

Spring Grove Mill — A mid-nineteenth-century mill occupied by George Mallinson & Sons, who moved here with 80 employees. By 1910 James Robinson and a separate firm of W H Robinson & Sons used this mill.

Longwood township

Cliff End Mill — Built in 1859 for Brook & Crosland, shoddy & mungo, who went bankrupt in 1862. Later used by Hanson & Co, which by 1890 became Hirst, Hanson & Co, then Hirst & Mallinson; now units some with textile use.

Dale Street Mill — A later mill of about the end of the nineteenth century. George Beaumont, woollen manufacturer, was here until the First World War together with J Hinchliffe & Co, shoddy & mungo.

Shires Yarns leased part of this mill just after the First World War.

Gosport Mill
John Sykes was in this mill in the 1860s. This firm developed into Edward Sykes & Sons, cotton spinners, who were here in 1910 and later part of the Hoyle group.

Imperial Mill
Small mill from the early twentieth century, built as a paper mill. Now used by Kangol Ltd, yarn spinners.

Parkwood Mill
J Broadbent & Sons and many others leased parts of this mill. 1906 the Longwood Finishing Company was formed and they remain there today. Some parts leased to smaller firms, but mainly Parkwood Mills Co Ltd.

Prospect Mill
Thomas Walker & Sons were here in the 1870s but *c.*1880 it was taken over by Joseph Hoyle, whose son became Sir Emmanuel Hoyle. This firm is said to have made 14 million yd of cloth for the army, 1914–18.

Quarmby Clough Mill
George Hattersley & Son worked this mill from the 1850s until it became part of Joseph Hoyle's group. In 1922 the mill collapsed.

Sunny Bank Mill
This is associated with the firm of C & J Hirst, which began in the 1870s as Crosland & Hirst. They were here to 1979, after which the mill stood empty for many years before being demolished to make way for housing.

Woodland Mill
According to the datestone, this was built in 1878. Occupied for many years by John Haigh & Sons Ltd and Job Beaumont & Sons up to the mid-1970s.

Marsden township

Bank Bottom Mill
A four-storey fulling mill built in 1824. Norris, Sykes & Fisher were there in the 1830s. It was later used by Ben Sykes & Sons before being bought by John Crowther. This has recently closed, and its future is uncertain.

Beehive Mill
Built by John Crowther at the end of the nineteenth century, it was occupied by Messrs R R Cook.

Capital Mill
See Clough Lee Mill.

Cellars Clough Mill
In the 1840s this was a cotton mill run by Dowse & Collins. It became a wool and worsted mill when Fisher Firth & Co moved in *c.*1890 – same family as S & C Hirst of Holme Mills, Marsden. Now units, including Textile Technical Services and Nuance Ltd, textile manufacturer.

Clough Lee Mill
A cotton mill from the 1790s, this was advertised for sale in 1810 when the owner was given as John Parkin, innkeeper.[35] Robinson Bros were here up to the First World War. The firm of J Bailly-Ancion Ltd had the mills after the Second World War to the late 1950s.

Fall Lane Mill	Originally leased by Isaac Bottomley in 1865. Henry Fisher & Co were there by 1899 but the old mill was demolished in 1903 to make way for new buildings.
Haigh Factory	This was an early cotton spinning mill. It caused some controversy because the owner, John Haigh, lived in London and used children from the Foundling Hospital in his mill. He went bankrupt in 1809, leaving the local parishes to take care of the orphan child workers.
Hey Green Mill	Originally a corn and fulling mill, it became one of the first mills to be run on a joint-stock basis by a number of clothiers.[36] It was subsequently used as a mill owner's residence and is now a restaurant.
Holme Mill	A Dartmouth estate mill from the end of the eighteenth century. FCR 1834 shows Scholes, Varley & Co, cotton spinners. It was later taken over by James Crowther & Sons, until S C Firth moved into the mill. Now industrial units with some textile use.
Kiln Croft Mill	This woollen mill is shown in 1854 close to Ottiwells Mill in Marsden.
Marsden Mill	Associated with John Edward Crowther.
New Mill	Another mill associated with the Crowther name – this time Crowther, Bruce & Co, who were in the mill up to the mid-twentieth century.
Old Isaac's Mill	See Fall Lane Mill.
Ottiwells Mill	This early scribbling mill will be forever associated with the Luddites and the murder of William Horsfall; now demolished.
Reedy or Ready Carr Mill	Used by John Edward Crowther; Robert Taylor & Co also leased part of this mill up to the 1890s.
Wood Bottom Mill	There are records of this mill being leased in 1794 and a connection with the Hirst family throughout the nineteenth century.

Milnsbridge township

Bank House Mill	FCR 1834 shows it being used as a woollen mill; by 1910, Ben Taylor & Sons, Angola and yarn spinners, were here.
Bottom Hall Mill	FCR 1834 shows Shaw, Eastwood & Taylor in this scribbling and carding mill, which was built *c.*1800. Hirst & Mallinson later moved into this mill and remained until the mid-twentieth century.
Bridge Croft Mill	Tom Hall & Co, Arnold Walker & Co and Sam Hurst, finisher, were here at the start of the twentieth century.
Britannia Mills	Messrs Shaw & Shaw, cotton spinners, used this mill from the end of the nineteenth century until the middle of the twentieth century.

Burdett Mill.

Burdett Mill	One of the group of mills used by Armitage Bros, from the Honley family. They went out of business in 1930 and the mill became part of the Crowther complex. Burdett Finishing Co were here after the Second World War. Now converted to flats.
Colne Vale Mill	Titus Calverley & Sons built this five-storey mill up a 'muddy track' at the end of the nineteenth century as well as a four-storey mill on the same site. Wright Mellor, Mayor of Huddersfield, was a director of this firm. Now demolished.
Commercial Mills	Middlemost Bros were here in the 1880s, then C & J Hirst took over c.1910 and stayed until 1979, when it closed. Now industrial units.

Elm Ing Mill	Sykes & Dyson were here in 1861 and became Joseph Dyson & Sons, which traded into the twentieth century.
George Street Mill	An old water-powered mill in the centre of Milnsbridge, this originally belonged to George Shires & Co, which became James Shires & Sons Ltd. The old mill was demolished and a new mill built, but the site is now a supermarket.
Quarmby Mill	See George Street Mill.
Spring Garden Mill	John Shaw & Bros came here in the 1860s. This firm later became George Shaw & Sons, cotton spinners; the firm of Ben Hall was in the mill about the Second World War, but it is now used by Pennine Blending Co Ltd.
Spring Mill	A two-storey mill built in 1831. FCR 1834 shows Armitage Bros already established here. By 1914 it was part of John Crowther's group.
Stafford Mills	Associated with James Sykes & Sons, who were here for the first half of the twentieth century.
Stanley Mills	Another of the Crowther Bros mills.
Stonefield Mill	The firm of Walker Dyson & Sons, woollen and worsted manufacturers, were in this mill from the 1870s to just after the First World War.
Union Mill	This is another of the mills associated with John Crowther.
Viaduct Mills	Fred Calverley & Co Ltd seem to have been here in 1910.
Whiteley Mill	See George Street Mill.

Slaithwaite township

Bank Gate Mill	One of the early mills on the Dartmouth estates. FCR 1834 shows J & J Farrar in the mill, whilst Wright Blackburn & Co were here in 1910.
Bank Gate Mill	See Brinks New Mill.
Bankfield Mill	This is referred to in 1910, when Albert Pearson, yarn spinner, was here, but there is no reference to the mill by the middle of the twentieth century.
Blackmoor Holm Mill	At Hill Top, a three-storey cotton mill built by Townend & Varley in 1796, leased for 42 years at £5 5/- p.a. with 8hp wheel, 38ft (11.6m) dia., water available 9 months.
Bottoms Mill	See Holt Mill.
Bridge Street Mill	Built about the 1870s, it was also known as Waterside Lane Mills. Joseph Brierley & Sons started in this mill until it was sold to J Pogson & Co in 1903, after a major fire. This firm remained in the mill for many years. It has now been demolished.
Brinks New Mill	Also known as Bank Gate Mill. Erected by E Eastwood above Blackmoor Mill at a rental of £10 10/- p.a.
Brook Mill	Also known as Crimble Mills. In the mid-nineteenth century this was a silk mill of William Wanklyn, then becoming a

woollen mill with George Haigh. In 1899, W & E Crowther spent some time in this mill. Now units with some textile use.

Clough House Mill
A small, three-storey scribbling mill built in the 1780s on the Dartmouth estate; leased in 1785 to Richard & Sarah Horsfall, who built a lower mill (Haywood Mill, known in 1828 as Lower Clough House Mill but disused by then). Known as Clough House Mill after Upper Clough House Mill shut, it was a water-powered woollen mill. In 1910 Edwin Shaw & Sons and Middlemost Bros, who stayed for over 50 years.

Clough Road Mill
Also sometimes called the Silk Mill, since that was the yarn first spun here. Built by Wanklin Bros of Manchester, it was taken over by Colne Valley Tweed Co.

Commercial Mill
Built in 1876 by Henry Walker, it was taken over in the 1890s by Pearson Brothers (see Victoria Mills, Golcar).

Crimble Clough Mill
Built in the 1870s for W & E Crowther.

Crimble Mills
See Brook Mills.

Globe Mill
Built by the Globe Worsted Spinning Co Ltd, established in 1886, this still dominates the centre of Slaithwaite. An overhead walkway joins mills on either side of the road.

Haywood Mill
See Clough House Mill.

Holt Mill
A very early mill on the Dartmouth estate. In 1785 Joseph Sykes of Upper and Holt Mill asked Lord Dartmouth for a loan of £100 to build a second scribbling mill. In 1790 he asked for a further advance for a dyehouse at Lower Holt Mill. Upper Mill burnt down on 5 October 1805. Lower Holt Mill was taken over by J Varley and ultimately converted to a brewery.

Lingards Mill
Possibly established as early as the sixteenth century, it was an early cotton mill, formerly a workshop, owned by Thomas Gartside on Dartmouth land.

Merrydale Mill
Upper Clough House; built by Richard Horsfall in 1785 on the Dartmouth Estate. It was one of the earliest scribbling mills in the Colne Valley.

Old Corn Mill
Built by John Varley on the Dartmouth estates as a scribbling mill, this was later occupied by Hirst & Brierley, which became Messrs Hirst Bros.

Platt Mill
By 1879 Beaumont & Bates were in this mill and stayed here for at least thirty years. A new mill was built on the same site when the first was damaged. Later, W E Cotton took over this mill.

Shaw Carr Wood Mill
See main text above.

Spa Mill
The Slaithwaite Spinning Co was established in this area in 1876/7 when No 1 mill was built on the site of earlier weaving sheds. No 2 mill followed in 1882, with No 3 in 1887. Spa Mill

Spa Mill with Globe Mill in the background.

itself was bought in 1902 and No 4 mill built in 1906. In the 1930s, it was sold for £12,760 to W H Robinson Ltd of Milnsbridge. The mill is now used by SKA Textiles and Spectrum Yarns.

Tag Mills — Used by W E Cotton & Sons, shoddy and mungo.

Upper Clough House Mill — See Clough House Mill.

Upper Mill — A scribbling and fulling mill built at the end of the eighteenth century by Messrs Shaw & Haigh on the Dartmouth estates. By 1910 James Holroyd & Son were here, with Elon Crowther spinning cotton in this mill in 1924. It is now units, including Kingfisher Weavers Ltd.

Water Side Mill — Dartmouth records show this mill burnt down in 1802, but was rebuilt; hence it is sometimes called Phoenix Mill. Varley, Eastwood & Co were in the mill at this time, but FCR 1834 shows Scott, Varley & Co, cotton spinners.

South Crosland township

Crosland Mill — An early cotton mill, in use about the end of the eighteenth century. FCR 1834 shows W W & H Stables, woollen manufacturer.

Notes

Chapter Two

1   Huddersfield Directory and Year Book, 1867.
2   *Ibid.*, 1873.
3   Huddersfield Trade Directory 1818.
4   *Huddersfield Weekly Examiner*, 13 Jul 1872.
5   *Ibid.*, 20 Sep and 4 Oct 1873.
6   *Ibid.*, 4 Feb 1882.
7   *Ibid.*, 22 Sep 1894.
8   Huddersfield Trade Directory 1900.
9   KC100/3.
10 W B Crump and G Ghorbal, *History of the Huddersfield Woollen Industry*, 1st edn 1935 (repr. by Kirklees Council Leisure Services, 1988).
11 Yorkshire Textile Directories [YTD].
12 KC100/3.
13 *Huddersfield Daily Examiner*, 4 and 18 Nov 1961.
14 *Ibid.*, 5 Feb 1963.
15 *Ibid.*, 21 Dec 1963.
16 Author's own inspection in August 2003.
17 White's Directory 1853.
18 Registry of Deeds, TK 432 627, Thornhill to Hall, 1856.
19 Charlton & Anderson Directory of Leeds, Huddersfield and Dewsbury, 1864.
20 *Huddersfield Weekly Examiner*, 25 Jul 1863.
21 Huddersfield Directory and Year Book, 1868.
22 *Ibid.*, 1873.
23 Huddersfield and District Directory, 1879; Deed 777 366 419 3-1877, Portland Mill, further mortgage.
24 *Huddersfield Daily Examiner*, 'Huddersfield in Industry' series, 1934.
25 *Huddersfield Examiner*, 27 Oct 1866, p. 4.
26 *Huddersfield Chronicle*, 2 Mar 1867.
27 *Ibid.*, 7 Jul 1883.
28 Cumberworth Parish Records.
29 1841 Census, 1277/03/9.
30 Kirkburton Parish records.
31 Registry of Deeds, Wakefield (1876 – 764 177 186).
32 Anon., *Industries of Yorkshire*, 1890, part 2, p. 92.

33 'Huddersfield as an Industrial Centre' – official handbook of Huddersfield Corporation, 1919.
34 *Huddersfield Daily Examiner*, 5 Dec 1942, obituary of Henry Peckett.
35 Registry of Deeds, Wakefield (1880 – 855 66 53).
36 *Ibid*. (1890 - 29 54 28).
37 *Ibid*. (42 974 443 20/10/1897 and 28 453 228 5/7 1900).
38 Education Year Book 1916.
39 *Huddersfield Daily Examiner*, 21 Jan 1932.
40 S/PLT/F2/5, Power Loom Tuners' Day Book, 1920.
41 *Huddersfield Daily Examiner*, 11 Aug 1970.
42 *Huddersfield Chronicle*, 12 Mar 1864.
43 Registry of Deeds, Wakefield (YM 164 193).
44 1841 Census.
45 Registry of Deeds, Wakefield (QK 249 271).
46 *Huddersfield Chronicle*, Mar 1864.
47 Deed 705 157 184, Liddell to Martin, 1874.
48 *Huddersfield Weekly Examiner*, 8 May 1875.
49 *Huddersfield Chronicle*, 13 Jun 1874.
50 1881 Census.
51 Records of Huddersfield Technical College.
52 B/An/66.
53 W. Yorks. Archives, Kirklees (S/NUDBTS/66).
54 Yorkshire Textile Directories 1910–1980.
55 *Huddersfield Daily Examiner*, 28 Oct 1980.
56 *Ibid*., 25 Jan 1972.
57 *Huddersfield Daily Examiner* – Huddersfield in Industry series No 1.
58 *Huddersfield Daily Examiner*, 24 Mar 1981.
59 *Ibid*., 21 Jul 1992.
60 Planning application 03/62/90741/W2.
61 *Huddersfield Weekly Examiner*, 13 Jan 1877.
62 *Huddersfield Chronicle*, 7 Sep 1867.
63 *Ibid*., 12 Jan 1867.
64 *Huddersfield Examiner*, Jan 1853.
65 *Huddersfield Chronicle*, 7 Sep 1867.

Chapter Three
1 Wakefield Deeds (KU 606 598).
2 *Huddersfield Chronicle*, 2 Mar 1867.
3 *Huddersfield & Holmfirth Examiner*, 25 Apr 1857.
4 *Huddersfield Chronicle*, 3 Oct 1857.
5 *Ibid*., 31 Oct 1857.
6 *Huddersfield Weekly Examiner*, 12 Sep 1874.
7 *Ibid*., 4 Jun 1881.
8 DD/R/dd/vii/69, West Yorkshire Archives, Kirklees.
9 *Huddersfield Daily Examiner*, 19 Jul 1884.
10 *Ibid*.
11 Handwritten note held by Mrs M S Glendinning.
12 *Huddersfield Daily Examiner*, 22 Jul 1935.

13 *Ibid.*, 15 Mar 1879.

14 *Ibid.*, 21 Jun 1883.

15 W Eastwood.

16 *Huddersfield Daily Examiner*, 4 Apr 1961.

17 *Ibid.*, 22 Sep 1964.

18 J Walters.

19 *Huddersfield Daily Examiner*, 8 Feb 1966.

20 D R H Williams, *Textile Factory Organisation & Management*, Emmott & Co, 1934.

21 *Huddersfield Daily Examiner*, 16 Jul 1934.

22 *Ibid.*, 24 May 1941, obituary of Alfred Ernest Learoyd.

23 *Ibid.*, 29 Aug 1959.

24 *Ibid.*, 28 Sep 1988.

25 *Ibid.*, 31 Jul 1964 and 26 Jan 1972.

26 *Ibid.*, 28 Sep 1973.

27 *Ibid.*, 30 Jul 1964.

28 Huddersfield Fine Worsteds Ltd, 13 Dec 1979.

29 *Huddersfield Daily Examiner*, 27 Aug 1980.

30 *Ibid.*, 13 May 1994.

31 *Huddersfield Weekly Examiner*, 10 Jan 1852.

32 *Ibid.*

33 Joseph Johnson, *Annals of Yorkshire*, 1860 (ed. John Mayhall), Vol. 1.

34 *Ibid.*

35 YTD 1910–1950.

36 *Huddersfield Weekly Examiner*, 15 Aug 1882.

37 *Ibid.*, 20 Jan 1848.

38 Healders & Twisters Union, S/HHT/12.

39 Joseph Johnson, *Annals of Yorkshire*, 1860 (ed. John Mayhall), Vol. 1.

Chapter Four

1 Registry of Deeds, KP 45 48 1829; KP 45 49 1829.

2 *Leeds Mercury*, 8 Apr 1848.

3 *Ibid.*, 10 Nov 1849.

4 Registry of Deeds, QK 727 820 1849.

5 *Leeds Mercury*, 26 May 1849.

6 *Ibid.*, 16 Feb 1850.

7 W B Crump and G Ghorbal, *History of the Huddersfield Woollen Industry*, 1st edn 1935 (repr. by Kirklees Council Leisure Services, 1988).

8 DD/RE/115/87 and 117/138 Leases.

9 *Huddersfield Weekly Examiner*, 19 Aug 1882.

10 Education Year Book 1916.

11 W. Yorks. Archives, KC315 Day.

12 *Huddersfield Daily Examiner*, 19 Jul 1977.

13 *Ibid.*, 9 Sep 1980.

14 Article from Anon., *Nostalgic Huddersfield*, True North Books, 2000.

15 KC799/5/8 Kenyon papers, W. Yorks. Archives.

16 *Huddersfield Daily Examiner*, 29 May 1954.

17 KC799/1/9, return of males over military age 1917.

18 SI 338 391, Brown to Kenyon, Registry of Deeds.

19 KC799/3/1, Kenyon *v.* Denby & Cumberworth UDC 1932.
20 KC799/6/1, Wages Book.
21 Reminiscences of W W Kenyon.
22 KC799/14/2, Wesleyan Methodist Circuits.
23 KC799/12/11, Misc. papers.
24 *Huddersfield Daily Examiner*, 24 Sep 1940.
25 *Ibid.*, 18 Feb 1975.
26 *Ibid.*, 12 and 17 May 1977.
27 West Yorkshire Archives, KC312/1/1.
28 *Ibid.*
29 Registry of Deeds, YL 457 469 1865 and ZG 563 643, 1866.
30 Registry of Deeds, 623 632 736, 1869.
31 Registry of Deeds, 1878 – 807 446 526.
32 Registry of Deeds, 1903 – 10 563 244.
33 Ainley Family Papers, KC312/1/1.
34 *Ibid.*
35 Registry of Deeds, 34 821 315 – 1909.
36 Booklet on Duke of York's visit to Kirkheaton Mills, 1932.
37 *Huddersfield Daily Examiner*, 10 Jan 1964.
38 *Ibid.*, 28 Jun 1968.
39 KC313/6/L.
40 KC313/6/2.
41 KC313/6/3.
42 KC311/20/8.
43 KC313/6/2.
44 *Huddersfield Chronicle*, 25 Jun 1864.
45 *Huddersfield Weekly Examiner*, 8 Feb 1873.
46 KC313/6/3.
47 *Ibid.*
48 YTD 1910–1950.
49 White's Trade Directory 1837, Vol. 2.
50 *Huddersfield Chronicle*, 29 Jun 1867.
51 *Ibid.*
52 *Huddersfield Weekly Examiner*, 23 Feb 1878.

Chapter Five

1 *Huddersfield Weekly Examiner*, 2 Jul 1853.
2 Wakefield Registry, PE 492 500.
3 Wakefield Registry, RU 692 781 2.1853.
4 *Huddersfield Daily Examiner*, 20 Jul 1901.
5 *Ibid.*, 10 Apr 1880.
6 *Ibid.*, 2 Feb 1993.
7 *Ibid.*, 15 Oct 1993.
8 WYK 1122/7/19 Royal Commission of Historical Monuments – Yorkshire Textile Mills Survey.
9 QE13/2/2, Land Tax Returns, Austonley.
10 Newsome Parish Church Magazine, 1885.
11 White's Trade Directory 1853.

12 *Huddersfield Weekly Examiner*, 13 Jul 1872.

13 *Ibid.*, 4 Oct 1873.

14 *Ibid.*, 19 Sep 1874.

15 *Ibid.*, 4 Nov 1876.

16 *Ibid.*, 12 Apr 1977.

17 KC51, Taylor & Littlewood papers.

18 KC67/2, Cloth Pressers' Society records.

19 KC51, 1917 pattern book.

20 *Huddersfield Weekly Examiner*, 9 Jan 1877.

21 *Huddersfield Chronicle*, 2 Jun 1866.

22 *Huddersfield Daily Examiner*, 12 Aug 1977.

23 *Ibid.*, 14 Jul 1978.

24 *Ibid.*, 16 Jun 1981.

25 *Ibid.*, 20 Jun 1996.

26 *Huddersfield Chronicle*, 12 Jan 1861.

27 *Huddersfield Weekly Examiner*, May 1875.

28 *Huddersfield Examiner*, 2 Jul 1853.

29 *Huddersfield Chronicle*, 26 Sep 1863.

30 *Huddersfield Weekly Examiner*, 22 Jul 1882.

Chapter Six

1 KC 311/14/16.

2 KC311/14/7.

3 Will of Hugh Ramsden, 1789.

4 Registry of Deeds, XY 736 881.

5 *Huddersfield Weekly Examiner*, 13 Aug 1853.

6 Registry of Deeds, XY 736 881.

7 *Huddersfield Weekly Examiner*, 29 May 1875.

8 Registry of Deeds, 764 618 696.

9 Registry of Deeds, 842 662 755.

10 *Huddersfield Daily Examiner*, 9 Mar 1976.

11 Registry of Deeds, 1920 – 93 29 12.

12 *Huddersfield Daily Examiner*, 25 Jun 1979.

13 *Ibid.*, 6 Dec 1983.

14 *Ibid.*, 23 Sep 1988.

15 British Parliamentary papers; Factory Commission Inquiries 1834; Part ii, vol. 5, C1 No. 262.

16 *Huddersfield Weekly Examiner*, 22 Apr 1876.

17 Yorkshire Textile Directories 1910–1950.

18 Registry of Deeds, 1917 – 20 437 167.

19 *Huddersfield Weekly Examiner*, 10 May 1884.

20 *Ibid.*, 23 April 1873.

21 *Colne Valley Guardian*, 29 Sep 1972.

22 *Huddersfield Weekly Examiner*, 26 Aug 1887.

23 *Ibid.*, 8 Dec 1970.

24 *Ibid.*, 23 Mar 1973.

25 *Ibid.*, 30 Nov 1976.

26 *Ibid.*, 20 Jun 1978.

27 J & C Haigh.

28 *Huddersfield Daily Examiner*, 11 Aug 1979.

29 *Ibid.*, 15 Oct 1980.

30 *Ibid.*, 10 Oct 1984.

31 *Ibid.*, 21 Apr 1988.

32 *Ibid.*, 24 Jun 1994.

33 *Ibid.*, 23 Mar 2001.

34 *Ibid.*, 4 Feb 1977.

35 *Leeds Mercury*, 10 Feb 1810.

36 M T Wild, 'An historical geography of the West Yorkshire textile industries to 1850', unpublished thesis, Birmingham University 1972.

Bibliography

Addy J ed, 1974, *A History of Denby Dale UDC*, E Walker & Sons.

Anon., 1890, *Industries of Yorkshire*, pts 1 & 2, Historical Publishing Co.

Anon., 1911, *A Manual of Cloth Finishing*, Heywood & Co.

Benson A P, 1983, *Textile Machines*, Shire Publications Ltd booklet, repr. 2002.

Bentley P, 1947, *Colne Valley Cloth*, Huddersfield & District Woollen Export Group.

Bradford Art Galleries & Museums, 1983, *Woollen or Worsted: An Introduction to Wool Processing*.

Brook R, 1968, *The Story of Huddersfield*, MacGibbon Kee Ltd.

Brooke A J, 1995, *A Catalogue of Textile Mills 1790–1914*, privately published, revd edn.

Burnham D K, 1980, *Warp & Weft: A Textile Terminology*, Royal Ontario Museum.

Busfield D, 1988, *Job Definitions and Inequality*, privately published.

Clarke B, 1980, *History of Lockwood & North Crosland*, privately published.

Crump W B, 1988 reprint, *Highways down the Ages*, Kirklees Leisure Services.

Crump W B & Ghorbal G, 1935, reprinted 1988, *History of the Huddersfield Woollen Industry*, Kirklees Leisure Services.

Giles C and Goodall A H, 1992, *Yorkshire Textile Mills 1770–1930*, HMSO.

Haigh E A ed, 1992, *Huddersfield: A Most Handsome Town,* Kirklees Cultural Services.

Heaton H, 1965, *Yorkshire Wool & Worsted Industry*. OUP.

Hind J R, 1948, *Woollen & Worsted Raw Materials*, Ernest Benn Ltd.

Huddersfield Corporation, 1919, *Huddersfield as an Industrial Centre*, Official Handbook of Huddersfield Corporation.

Hudson P, 1986, *Genesis of Industrial Capital*, CUP.

Hughes J, 1851, *History of the Township of Meltham*, John Russell Smith, London.

Humberstone G, *The Woollen Industry of Huddersfield District and its relation to local Geography 1750–1925*, Thesis; MA Geography.

Hummel J J, 1893, *The Dyeing of Textile Fabrics*, Cassell & Co.

Jagger M A, 1914, *History of Honley*, A Jubb & Sons.

Lipson E, 1956, *The History of the Woollen & Worsted Industry*, Frank Cass, London.

Minter G & E, 2000, *Discovering Old Huddersfield*, H Barden & Co., pt 4.

Morehouse H J, 1984, *History of the Parish of Kirkburton*, privately published.

Phillips G S, 1848, *Walks around Huddersfield*, privately published.

Piggott S, 1949, *A Study of Industry*, Wm Hollins & Co.

Reach A B, 1849, republished 2001, *A Green and Shoddy Land*, Northern Line Design.

Redmonds G, 1982, *The Heirs of Woodsome*, G. R. Books.

Redmonds G, 1985, *Changing Huddersfield*, privately published.

Shackleton Esme, 1998, *Yorkshire Snippets*, Peaceprint.

Sykes D F E, 1988, *History of the Colne Valley*, privately published.

Williams D R H, 1934, *Textile Factory Organisation & Management*, Emmott & Co.

Aspects Series

The Aspects series is a collection of independently penned studies relating to the Yorkshire district, which offers the reader a wide variety of topics ranging from seventeenth-century misdemeanours to late twentieth-century childhood memories. Aspects, in the care of Wharncliffe Publishing Limited, continues to provide opportunities for writers and local historians to see their efforts assembled and presented in an accessible publication. Some of the following titles are included in this series.

Aspects of Huddersfield
Isobel Schofield
ISBN 1-871647-66-5
£9.95

Aspects of Huddersfield 2
Stephen Wade
ISBN 1-903425-23-9
£9.99

Aspects of Bradford
Bob Duckett
ISBN 1-871647-55-X
£9.95

Aspects of Bradford 2
Bob Duckett
ISBN 1-871647-82-7
£9.95

Aspects of Calderdale
John Billingsley
ISBN 1-903425-20-4
£9.99

Aspects of Leeds 2
Lynne Stevenson Tate
ISBN 1-871647-59-2
£9.95

Aspects of Leeds 3
Lynne Stevenson Tate
ISBN 1-903425-05-0
£9.99

The Making of Huddersfield
Dr George Redmonds
ISBN 1-903425-39-5
£9.99

The Making of the West Yorkshire Landscape
Anthony Silson
ISBN 1-903425-31-X
£9.99

WHARNCLIFFE BOOKS
47 Church Street – Barnsley – South Yorkshire – S70 2AS
Tel: 01226 734555 – 734222 Fax: 01226 72443 E-mail: enquiries@pen-and-sword.co.uk
Website: www.wharncliffebooks.co.uk